What are educators saying about Assertive Discipline?

Here's what teachers have to say:

"I feel Assertive Discipline techniques should be mandatory. They work and are multi-disciplinary."
— *Suzanne D. Hemminger; Teacher; Morgan Park High School; New Lenox, IL*

"We offer Assertive Discipline through our county organization of 9,500 members. We get consistent raves. The accolades are fantastic. The results are 100% positive!"
— *Joanne Palladino; President; Camden County Council of Education Associations*

"I just feel that kids are much happier when they know what's expected of them—when they don't have to guess what a teacher's reaction to their behavior will be. There's security in being able to predict your environment. That's one of the biggest advantages of Assertive Discipline."
— *Melba Jean Boyd; Teacher/Family and School Coordinator; Metropolitan Nashvillle Public Schools; Nashville, TN*

"School has been in session for four weeks now and I cannot believe the difference. I have had no discipline problems at all. The kids are great, and I go home feeling happy and validated. I actually have time to teach English this year! People who walk into my classroom think the students have somehow changed, but I know it's really *me* that has changed."
— *Joyce Milburn; Teacher; Discovery Christian School; Anaheim, CA*

Here's what school superintendents have to say:

"As a school administrator, I have total confidence in the track record of the Assertive Discipline program. It has given us a base that we didn't have. Assertive Discipline has set us in the right direction in looking at a child's self-esteem as the key issue in student discipline."
— *Ray Tolcacher; Superintendent; Windsor School District; Windsor, CA, Past President Association of California School Administrators (ACSA)*

"Assertive Discipline is a widely used method of establishing a positive school climate. With consistent follow up, staffs are able to maintain the momentum of the initial success and establish an atmosphere conducive to learning."
— *Saul B. Grossmann, Ed.D.; Southeast Region Superintendent; School District of Philadelphia; Philadelphia, PA*

"I have found Assertive Discipline to be one of the most consistent approaches to discipline. It has proven to be extremely helpful in the area of classroom management for our experienced teachers and, even more so, for newly licensed teachers. What I like most about the program is that it gets students to think about the consequences of their actions. This thoughtful process will go a long way in building character and making responsible citizens of our students.
— *Felton M. Johnson; Community Superintendent; Community School District Nine; New York City Public Schools; Bronx, NY*

Here's what principals have to say:

"This program is fantastic. Within weeks after its implementation, my staff was amazed and delighted with the positive changes in our children's behavior."
— *Dr. Sharon Lockett; Principal; Woodward Elementary School; Kalamazoo, MI*

"Assertive Discipline provides the common vocabulary, techniques and plan that enable all our teachers to work together on our common goal: educating all students to their potential. Behavior management is no longer someone else's responsibility. Our teachers are in charge."
— *Kimiko Fukuda; Principal; Woodrow Wilson Academy of International Studies; San Diego, CA*

"Assertive Discipline removes needless anxiety for the classroom teacher. Classroom management becomes routine. My teachers are freed to do what they do best—teach!"
— *Mike LaRaus; Principal; Laurence Brock School; East Brunswick, NJ*

"According to an old African proverb, '*It takes an entire village to educate a child.*' Assertive Discipline helps the entire community realize the responsibility placed on parents, teachers, administrators and students. Our goal is to build strong, self-reliant, self-educating young people. Assertive Discipline is a major building block—it gets the results we seek."
— *Larry Biddle; Assistant Principal; Conway High School; Conway, SC*

"Responsible choices are vital for our children. Assertive Discipline supports self-esteem and responsibility. It provides positive reinforcement in a clear, concise, understandable manner for teacher and student."
— *Joyce Klevence; Former Principal; Blessed Sacrament School; St. Paul, MN*
  NCEA Distinguished Principal 1991

Here's what teacher educators have to say:

"We are excited about the five years we have worked with the Canter organization. The quality of the courses we have offered has met all of our expectations. Canter programs have allowed the teachers in the field to receive the application of the theoretical base for their very real practical situations. Thank you for your willingness to work with us in providing a quality educational program for our students and the teachers in the state of Arizona. Assertive Discipline makes a real difference in education."
— *Dr. Patty J. Horn; Dean; Grand Canyon University; Phoenix, AZ*

"I have found Assertive Discipline to be the most eclectic program of any discipline model I have studied or used. It is a positive and dignified approach to classroom management and discipline, and the major strength of Assertive Discipline's approach is the development of self-discipline in students. At Baylor we have incorporated the Canter model into our teacher training program. I have personally trained in Assertive Discipline and teach these skills to new and experienced teachers in workshops and accredited courses."
— *Elden R. Barrett, Ph.D; Chairman of the Department of Clinical and Field Experiences; Baylor University; Waco, TX*

LEE CANTER'S

ASSERTIVE DISCIPLINE®

POSITIVE BEHAVIOR MANAGEMENT
FOR TODAY'S CLASSROOM

**By Lee Canter
and Marlene Canter**

Senior Editor
Marcia Shank

Contributing Editor
Bob Winberry

Editorial Staff
Jacqui Hook
Carol Provisor
Pat Sarka
Barbara Schadlow
Kathy Winberry

Design
The Arcane Corporation

Cover Photo
Bob Winberry

©1992 Lee Canter & Associates
P.O. Box 2113, Santa Monica, CA 90407-2113
800-262-4347 310-395-3221

Printed in the United States of America
First printing March 1992

96 95 94 93   11 10 9 8 7 6 5 4 3

Library of Congress Catalog Card Number 92-071250
ISBN 0-939007-45-2

DEDICATION

To Kathy Winberry

Our colleague.
Our friend.

For your infinite wisdom;
for your tireless dedication;
and for your passion for wanting to
help educators be the very best they can be.

Thank you for joining us 13 years ago
and for working side by side with us
to make this a better world
for all of our children.

Lee and Marlene

CONTENTS

SECTION ONE: THE ASSERTIVE ATTITUDE

SECTION TWO: YOUR CLASSROOM DISCIPLINE PLAN

SECTION THREE: TEACHING RESPONSIBLE BEHAVIOR

SECTION FOUR: DIFFICULT STUDENTS

FORWARD

Look again at the cover of this book. The children you see gathered around Lee Canter are not professional models—they are students at Will Rogers Elementary School in Santa Monica, California. I am their principal, and Lee is one of many volunteer tutors from Lee Canter & Associates who have become an integral part of our school family.

Lee Canter & Associates is our "adopt-a-school" partner, and as such is providing a unique form of support to both our staff and our students.

Recognizing that the education of children is the responsibility of the entire community, Lee and Marlene Canter have committed themselves, and their firm, to a long-term relationship with our school. This relationship includes not only continuing financial support, but, more importantly, person-to-person relationships. Each week twenty Canter staff members come to school to mentor students who need both academic tutoring *and* a positive adult role model. The Canter volunteers effectively serve in this capacity.

We have seen many changes in the attitude and behavior of the students who have had the opportunity to participate in this program. The effects of this program have been remarkable.

Our school's partnership with Lee Canter & Associates is especially meaningful to me because it represents the continuation of a relationship that began in the early 1970s when I first met Lee.

At that time I was a teacher in the Lennox School District in Lennox, California. This small unincorporated area adjacent to the Los Angeles airport was a port of entry for many immigrant families. It was an area characterized by a high crime rate, and the majority of our students' families lived below the poverty level. Concerned about the poor discipline in many of the classrooms, the superintendent of the district decided to institute districtwide a new behavior management program, Lee Canter's Assertive Discipline.

Consequently, over the period of a year, every administrator, teacher and classified staff member of the Lennox school district was trained in the Assertive Discipline techniques. As a teacher I attended several workshops that were taught by Lee Canter, and I successfully integrated the behavior management techniques I learned into my own classroom. To augment our classroom efforts, every school developed a discipline philosophy that was adopted schoolwide.

During that year the district was transformed from one in which many students were uncontrolled and uncontrollable, to one in which teachers were able to spend their time educating their students rather than disciplining them. Today Lennox continues to be a model district where children attend schools that are islands of calm amid a community that is often locked in crisis.

In the years that ensued I often ran into Lee at various conferences and maintained a professional relationship with him. So it was to my great delight when, during my first week on the job as principal at Will Rogers, I learned that our school had been "adopted" by a local business, Lee Canter & Associates. I was thrilled to have the opportunity to work together with Lee Canter again—this time to develop an innovative relationship between school and community which I feel has the potential of changing the face of education as it now exists.

Today, the staff and parents at Will Rogers share a common vision:

We are committed to making sure that every student at Will Rogers is routinely exposed to powerful learning experiences.

We are committed to seeing that all of our students develop into lifelong learners and contributors to society.

We know that we can accomplish these goals only with the caring dedication of the entire local community. Lee Canter and Marlene Canter, together with the staff of Lee Canter & Associates, play a significant role in this quest. We gratefully acknowledge their contributions to the future citizens of the next century.

Juli DiChiro
Principal,
Will Rogers Elementary School
Santa Monica, California

PREFACE

The original Assertive Discipline text was written fifteen years ago. Throughout these years we've stayed in close contact with teachers who have been using our program. We've listened to their questions and concerns, we've addressed their problems and shared their successes.

Our constant contact with teachers, along with our continuing research, has allowed us to clarify what works best in Assertive Discipline. It's also given us the opportunity to adjust the program to meet the changing needs of teachers and students.

Into this revised text, therefore, we've incorporated what we've learned—what works best in Assertive Discipline. We've also answered the questions that have come up over the years.

The goal of the revised Assertive Discipline is to teach students to choose responsible behavior and in so doing raise their self-esteem and increase their academic success.

Teachers who have used Assertive Discipline before will discover a greater, more in-depth approach to classroom behavior management and to meeting the needs of individual students. Teachers new to Assertive Discipline will find a behavior management program that will help them confidently create an optimal classroom environment conducive to learning.

It is our hope that all teachers will find within this text the skills that will empower them to meet their own professional goals and the needs of their students.

ACKNOWLEDGMENTS

This book would not exist without the care and dedication of many wonderful individuals who are near and dear to us. To these friends and colleagues we extend our heartfelt thanks and appreciation. Your continued support has made this book possible.

To those of our consultants who have given us valuable input and feedback on how to revise this text: Barbara Akst, Elden Barrett, Harriett Burt, Judy Cooper, Jim Currens, Diana Day, Sandra Grey, Mike LaRaus, David Losey, Betty Minor, Carolyn Reedom, Janet Robinson, Vic Schneidman, Sandi Searls and Bert Simmons.

To Kathy Winberry and Barbara Schadlow for providing the honest and creative feedback that so improved the quality of this work.

To Tom Lasley, Joan McClintic, Barbara Huff and Lil Mikelman for the care and interest they gave in critiquing the final manuscript.

To Debbie Runzler and Mary Ann Vollrath for all the hours they spent transcribing the manuscript.

To Pat Sarka, Carol Provisor and Jacqui Hook—the editorial staff—for all the diligent work they contributed to this project.

To Tom Winberry and Bob Winberry for the graphic design that communicates our words with such clarity and readability.

And most importantly, to Marcia Shank and Bob Winberry: Thank you both for your endless patience and dedication that made this book more than it ever would have been without you!

Santa Monica, California   Lee and Marlene Canter
March 1992

INTRODUCTION
by Marlene Canter

It was the summer of 1968 when I first met Lee. We were in college and Lee knew exactly what he wanted to be—a teacher. He wanted to make a difference with kids, to bring history alive for them in the classroom. I also knew exactly what I wanted to be—a social worker. I wanted to help children feel the best about themselves and help them reach their full potential.

In 1970 when Lee and I married, the social consciousness movement of the 60s helped inspire us to make our values and ideals a part of our plans for the future: We wanted to make a difference in the lives of children. By this time, Lee was in graduate school at the University of Southern California working on his masters degree in social work. I was at Pacific Oaks Teachers College working on my teaching credentials and advanced special education training. Lee had decided that social work would allow him to influence the lives of people in a different way than teaching would. I had decided that teaching would allow me to be closer to the children that I wanted to help.

We spent the next several years pursuing our individual professions. After a few years in social work, Lee began to focus his career on school consultation and teacher training. I was teaching special education while continuing to study child development and special education techniques.

It was during this time that Assertive Discipline was born.

There was a child in my class whose disruptive behavior challenged me to look for new techniques that would help him reach the potential I knew he had, and to succeed in school.

Together, Lee and I began to research the problems of discipline in the classroom and the methods that successful teachers were using in dealing with these problems.

Through this research, and augmented by our own experiences, we began to develop a behavior management model that was based on consistency, follow through and positive relationship-building. As we worked with my student, it became apparent to us that, when given clear expectations and consistent follow through, most children, even the very disruptive ones, are able to choose appropriate behavior, thereby increasing their opportunities for greater success in school.

This realization, along with our continuing research of effective teachers, became the core of the Assertive Discipline program.

As we began to share our techniques with other teachers, we saw that our newly developed approach was vitally needed in many classrooms. We discovered that although teachers were well trained in teaching techniques, they often lacked the extra skills necessary to deal with the daily behavior challenges they faced.

In 1976 we published our first book—*Assertive Discipline: A Take-Charge Approach for Today's Educator*. Our goal was to help teachers learn to "take charge" of the classroom in a firm and positive manner.

Over the years, as we have continued to work with teachers, we have expanded and built upon the basic behavior management principles presented in our original work. Today's teachers face even more complex situations than when we began our program and need an even more comprehensive model. In response, Assertive Discipline has continued to evolve.

The revised Assertive Discipline that we present in this book will enable you to go beyond "taking charge" of the classroom. We feel that it is vital that we work together to prevent behavior problems from occurring and to teach children to make responsible decisions regarding their behavior.

It is our belief that by enabling children to be successful in school we are empowering them with the skills that will become the foundation for their self-esteem and future success.

Throughout the past 16 years Lee and I have been surrounded by many caring and talented educators who have worked side by side with us to develop and deliver a wide range of programs to teachers. All of us share a passion for making a difference in the lives of children, and it is this passion that has guided our decisions and given us enormous satisfaction.

On behalf of Lee, our dedicated staff and our Canter consulting associates, this revised edition of *Assertive Discipline* carries with it our continuing commitment to provide educators with the resources necessary to increase their effectiveness in the classroom. Each day our work with educators and parents reminds us how honored we are to do the work we do and to be able to make a difference in the lives of children. It is our hope that this newly revised edition of *Assertive Discipline* provides dedicated teachers like yourself with the tools necessary to create a positive and productive classroom environment.

THE
ASSERTIVE
ATTITUDE

THE ASSERTIVE ATTITUDE

As a teacher, you want the optimal classroom environment in which you can teach and your students can learn. To create this environment, you must increase your ability to influence your students to behave, in spite of the problems you face at school, and in spite of the problems students bring with them to school.

To increase your influence, you must become what we call an assertive teacher. In this first section of *Assertive Discipline*, we will take a close look at the assertive attitude—what it is and how you can incorporate it into your teaching style.

In Chapter 1 we will look at your own rights and responsibilities as a teacher, and the outside influences that might be affecting your success in the classroom. In Chapter 2 we will look at the negative expectations that might actually be hampering your behavior management efforts.

Finally, in Chapter 3, we will set the stage for the rest of the book by examining the three response styles that teachers use in their interactions with students. You will see here that response styles are important predictors of how you relate to students, and of how students respond to you.

THE EMPOWERED TEACHER

You have the right to teach and your students have the right to learn in a classroom free from disruptive behavior—a classroom that both reflects your own behavioral expectations *and* creates an atmosphere in which student self-esteem can flourish.

To create this learning environment, remember that:

- You have the right and the responsibility to establish rules and directions that clearly define the limits of acceptable and unacceptable student behavior.

- You have the right and the responsibility to teach students to consistently follow these rules and directions throughout the school day and school year.

- You have the right and the responsibility to ask for assistance from parents and administrators when support is needed in handling the behavior of students.

And why are these rights and responsibilities so important?

If you are like many teachers today, you are having increasing difficulty establishing the classroom environment you need in which to teach and the classroom environment your students need in which to learn.

Why?

Discipline remains a key problem in education in the 90s.

All too often, teachers are confronted with students who talk when asked to be quiet; who dawdle when asked to work; who argue and talk back when asked to follow directions. The result: Invaluable teaching time is lost, student achievement and self-esteem drop, and teacher frustration increases.

Why are so many teachers having so much difficulty with students? Why do so many teachers feel powerless to influence students to behave appropriately?

What's happened?

To find the answers we need to look outside the classroom and beyond the school.

Respect

In the not-so-distant past, teachers were empowered with instant authority due to the simple fact that they were "the teacher." Society reinforced this authority by the high esteem in which it held educators. Parents reinforced this authority by stressing the importance of education and the importance of listening to the teacher.

In addition, parents warned their children about the consequences of misbehavior—and they backed their words with action. Children knew that if they got in trouble at school, they'd be in twice as much trouble at home. Consequently, a vast majority of children came to school with built-in respect for teachers and education. They came prepared to behave. They came prepared to learn. Behavior management, or discipline, usually consisted of nothing more than a teacher's stern look or a few well-chosen words. The simple promise of, "I will call your parents if you do that again" was sufficient to motivate most students, including the most disruptive ones, to behave.

In the past, teachers were empowered by the value placed on education by parents and society alike. Things are much different today. Today a teacher has to deal with society's lack of respect for teachers and the educational process in general. Today a teacher does not automatically have the respect of students and their parents.

What does this mean to you?

The discipline approaches of the past do not work with the students of the 90s.

Behavior Problems

Students today are bringing more than pens and pencils to school. In increasing numbers, they're bringing with them the confusion and uncertainties of broken homes, poverty, emotional and physical neglect and abuse, and the fact of life that too many of their parents are unwilling or unable to motivate them to succeed in school. The overwhelmed, often troubled adults in many of our students' lives cannot or will not take the time or make the effort necessary to teach their children to feel good about themselves, to have positive self-esteem or to develop the academic and behavior skills that will empower them to succeed in school as well as in life.

Children are not innately motivated to behave in school.

There are vital precursors that are necessary to ensure that a child succeeds. Loving attention and motivation from parents and family, a stable home environment, and a positive outlook toward society's possibilities are all necessary to help children develop the self-esteem and self-control needed to choose responsible behavior. Because more and more students do not have these prerequisites for success, the number of problems in our classrooms continues to multiply, and the burden placed on you, the teacher, increases.

One of our staff members, a recently retired teacher, summed it up well when he sighed and stated, "Is it any wonder so many children behave the way they do? After all, they come to school raised in what can best be described as an X-rated world."

These students, however, are still in your classroom, and more than ever need guidance, need concern, and need someone who is in the position to help them reach their full academic and social potential.

Behavior Management Training

Ironically, even though teachers are called upon to work with more and more students with more and more problems, as professionals they still receive minimal, if any, comprehensive training in behavior management. And often the training they receive can cause more harm than good. Here's why:

Most behavior management training that teachers receive is based upon contemporary theories of child psychology as the philosophies of doctors Freud, Skinner, Glasser and Dreikurs have been brought into the classroom. These philosophies have had a major impact upon contemporary education courses. The problem is, given the limited amount of time devoted to training in discipline, the concepts have been simplified, watered down, distorted and misinterpreted to the point that teachers have been misled to believe simplistic concepts such as:

> If you discipline a child for disruptive behavior you will cause him emotional distress.

> You must avoid conflicts with students. If a child severely disrupts the classroom, don't confront him. Find an alternative that will better meet his needs.

> You must understand the causes of a child's problem behavior. The child may be motivated by unconscious drives and cannot control her behavior.

> When a child is upset and disruptive, you need to help him express his feelings before you can ever get him to behave.

As a result of being minimally exposed to many different philosophies, teachers are often left questioning their disciplinary approaches:

> *"Have I been too hard on Mark?"*
>
> *"Should I counsel him before I call his parents?"*
>
> *"Should I be so strict with Stephanie? After all, she has emotional problems."*

This confusion does not lead to confident behavior management. Instead, guilt, anxiety and frustration can result from such self-questioning.

In addition, the exposure to so many different philosophies has resulted in the fact that there is no longer "one way" to run a classroom and teach students.

In the past, be it right or wrong, most teachers had the same basic disciplinary expectations of all students. They expected students to sit in their seats, work without talking, raise their hands and wait to be called upon to speak, and do assigned work when they were told to do it.

Today, expectations may vary greatly from teacher to teacher. They may range from those of the previously mentioned traditional teacher to those of teachers who are utilizing new approaches to learning, such as cooperative learning groups. These teachers obviously have different, and often more realistic, expectations for their students. They allow a great deal more interaction among students, emphasize the importance of students working in cooperation with their peers, and oftentimes involve their students in the decision-making process for how the classroom is run.

Different expectations among teachers result in fewer clear-cut, across-the-board standards of acceptable behavior. Students may complain, "My other teacher didn't make me do that. It's not fair!"

Thus, a teacher today may have greater difficulty in establishing standards and expectations in the classroom, and in communicating them to students who may be accustomed to a variety of standards set by other teachers.

The Myth of the Good Teacher

Another factor makes it difficult for you to get your needs met today. We call it the "myth of the good teacher." This myth basically goes as follows: A "good" teacher should be able to handle all behavior problems on her own and within the confines of the classroom.

The assumption is, if you are competent, you never need to go to your principal or the child's parents for assistance.

This myth was alive 15 years ago when the Assertive Discipline program was developed and, unfortunately, is still alive today.

This myth is nonsense. No teacher, no matter how skilled he is or how much experience or training she has, is capable of working successfully with each and every student without support. This myth is especially damaging today because of the increase in students whose behavior is so disruptive that a teacher *must* have assistance from the principal, the parent(s) and, if possible, a counselor, in order to deal effectively with unacceptable behavior.

The burden of guilt this myth places on a teacher is by no means trivial. According to the myth, if teachers were really competent they wouldn't have these problems. These guilt-ridden feelings of inadequacy tend to keep teachers from asking for the help they need and deserve. This is limiting and unproductive to all involved.

Curriculum

Many teachers have been taught that if their curriculum is first rate, they will have minimal classroom behavior problems. We agree that the better your curriculum and the more motivating, exciting and academically appropriate it is, the fewer behavior problems you will have. In fact, one of the best preventative behavior management tools is skilled academic teaching.

The problem, however, is that before your lessons ever begin, before you have the opportunity to pique your students' interest with motivating academic material, you must first have their attention. Your students must be seated. They must be quiet. And they must be listening to you.

Good curriculum will help students stay on task. But first they must know how to *be* on task.

The reality of the 90s is that you are going to have students who exhibit behavior problems even with the best of curriculums.

Looking at what we've covered so far, we see that:

- Teachers today do not receive the respect from parents and from society that teachers used to receive.

- More students come to school with behavior problems than ever before.

- Teachers are not sufficiently trained to deal with today's behavior problems.

- The myth of the good teacher keeps teachers from asking for the assistance they need.

- Good curriculum is not always enough to motivate students to behave.

All of these factors have combined to diminish a teacher's real or perceived ability to influence students' behavior. And that loss of influence has, in turn, made it more difficult for many teachers to effectively maintain discipline in the classroom.

As a teacher today, you must empower yourself to move past these problems and create the learning environment needed to guarantee your right to teach and your students' right to learn.

What do today's students need?

We've talked about your own rights and responsibilities that will help empower you in the classroom. Now, what are the rights of your students and what do your students need from you?

To grow academically, socially and emotionally, students need to be in a classroom in which a concerned teacher is willing and able to set consistent, positive behavioral limits while providing warmth and support to students for their appropriate behavior—to empower students with the skills to succeed.

Students need to know your behavioral expectations.

Students cannot be expected to guess how you want them to behave in all situations. If they are to succeed in your classroom, they need to know, without doubt, what you expect of them.

Students need limits.

When students are not given the limits they need, they will act up in order to make the adults around them take notice. A student's disruptive behavior is often a plea for someone to care enough to make him or her stop. In the classroom, that someone is you. Students need to know what behavior is expected of them. They then need to know what will occur if they choose not to comply with those expectations.

Students need positive recognition and support.

Students need to know you will recognize and support positive behavior just as you will limit inappropriate, disruptive behavior. Mutual trust and respect are established when students know they will get honest and consistent feedback from you. In exchange, you will get honest effort from them.

Students need to be taught how to choose responsible behavior.

Most importantly, students need you to take the time and make the effort to *teach* them how to choose responsible behavior. True success and increased self-esteem occur when students first learn how you expect them to behave, and then when they choose that behavior on their own.

This leap from simply following rules to *choosing* responsible behavior is imperative.

If students are to be successful in the real world they must be capable of making independent, responsible choices.

We find that students have these rights in the classroom:

- Students have the right to a teacher who will set firm and consistent limits.

- Students have the right to a teacher who will provide them with consistent positive encouragement to motivate them to behave.

- Students have the right to know what behaviors they need to engage in that will enable them to succeed in the classroom.

- Students have the right to a teacher who will take the time to teach them how to manage their own behavior.

Obviously students cannot establish these rights for themselves.

It's up to you to make the commitment to meet the needs of your students. And to be in a position to do so, you will need the skills and confidence to influence your students.

Positive, caring influence is the catalyst that communicates to students the importance you place on helping each and every one of them succeed. Your influence is the force that can decrease classroom disruptions, increase student self-esteem and, in so doing, help you meet your own professional needs.

How can you increase your influence in spite of all the problems that stand in your way? *By becoming a more assertive teacher.*

Let's take a look at what that means.

Assertive.

As found in Webster's dictionary, the verb "assert" can be defined as: "To state or affirm positively, assuredly, plainly or strongly."

We define an assertive teacher as "one who clearly and firmly communicates her expectations to her students, and is prepared to reinforce her words with appropriate actions. She responds to students in a manner that maximizes her potential to get her own needs to teach met, but in no way violates the best interest of the students."

Assertive teachers communicate their influence by sending a very clear message to their students:

"I am committed to being the leader in this classroom, a leader who will establish an environment where I can teach and my students can learn. To reach this goal, I am committed to teaching and empowering my students to choose the responsible behavior that will allow them to succeed in school, and to succeed later in life.

"I care too much about my responsibility as a teacher to allow disruptive behavior to stop me from teaching. I care too much about my students to allow them to behave in a manner that is not in their best interests."

By this commitment, an assertive teacher is empowered to reach his or her own professional goals, and in so doing to meet the needs of the students. Our goal in this book is to teach you the skills needed to become an assertive teacher, an empowered teacher—a teacher of influence.

CHAPTER ONE — KEY POINTS

The Empowered Teacher

- You have the right and responsibility to establish rules and directions that clearly define the limits of acceptable and unacceptable student behavior.

- You have the right and responsibility to teach students to consistently follow these rules and directions throughout the school day and school year.

- You have the right and responsibility to ask for assistance from parents and administrators when support is needed in handling the behavior of students.

- Students have the right to a teacher who will set firm and consistent limits.

- Students have the right to a teacher who will provide them with consistent positive encouragement to motivate them to behave.

- Students have the right to know what behaviors they need to engage in that will enable them to succeed in the classroom.

- Students have the right to a teacher who will take the time to teach them how to manage their own behavior.

CHAPTER TWO

ROADBLOCKS TO BEING ASSERTIVE

To become an assertive, more effective teacher, you will need to acquire skills that will enhance your influence with your students. But before we explore these skills, let's take a moment to identify and move you past a roadblock that just might be standing in your way.

What stops a teacher from being assertive?

What stops a teacher from creating a classroom free from disruptive behavior?

The answer may surprise you: In most instances, it's not the disruptive students.

The major roadblock to successful classroom management is a teacher's own negative expectations about her ability to deal with disruptive student behavior.

And this is especially true in relation to students with special needs—often those very students who do present the most extreme behavior problems.

When confronted with students with problems, teachers often lose track of the potential they really have to positively affect these students. And in so doing, they lose track of their own rights and responsibilities: *"I have the right to establish rules. I have the responsibility to teach all of my students to follow these rules. And I have the right to ask for assistance from parents and administrators."*

These teachers feel that there are circumstances beyond their control that prevent them from influencing these students in any positive manner. They feel that no matter what they may try, they really can't get these students to sustain appropriate behavior.

With difficult students, many teachers simply feel powerless.

Let's take a look now at some of the perceptions that stand in the way of many teachers' behavior management success.

Students' Emotional Problems

Many teachers believe that students who have emotional problems cannot control their behavior without the help of a psychologist or another professional trained to deal with these problems.

We often hear teachers make statements such as, "Jason needs professional help, and until he gets that help there is no way I can handle him."

Inadequate Parenting

Today we face more and more students who come from broken homes, homes torn apart by alcohol and drug abuse, and homes in which students may be neglected or even abused. Many teachers believe this deprivation at home is so harmful to students that the students cannot be expected to meet behavioral expectations at school.

It's not uncommon to hear teachers making comments such as, "Coming from a home like that, it's no wonder she has problems. What can you expect from her? She's never been given any guidance for how to behave."

Students Who Live in a Poverty Environment

The number of students raised in poverty is growing at an alarming rate. Some teachers feel that given the problems that students from lower socioeconomic backgrounds experience, they simply cannot be expected to meet the same behavioral guidelines as other students.

These teachers often make statements such as, "Living in this neighborhood, of course he gets into trouble all of the time," or "Children in that neighborhood have no respect for school or teachers. There is no way you can get him to listen to you without screaming or punishing."

Students with Special Needs

More special education students and students with learning disabilities are being mainstreamed into regular classrooms than ever before. It is not uncommon to find teachers who believe they cannot deal with the behavior of students with special needs in a regular classroom. We often hear statements such as, "I can't handle his behavior. He needs to be in a classroom with a teacher trained to deal with his problems."

Emotional problems, inadequate parenting, poverty, and special education needs are certainly real problems that can and will make it more difficult for students to behave appropriately.

The roadblock to these students' success, however, is a teacher's doubts about his or her ability to help students in spite of these problems.

What you will learn in this book is that given the proper skills, these problems, or any others, do not have to prevent you from positively impacting student behavior. Every chapter you read will diminish your self-doubt by giving you specialized techniques that all students will respond to, even the most disruptive ones.

But before you can successfully implement these skills, you must first be convinced of one vital fact:

Most children <u>can</u> behave when they want to do so.

Regardless of inadequate parenting, regardless of poverty, regardless of emotional problems and regardless of special education needs, most students can behave.

Bottom line, you must believe that if students don't behave, it's because they've chosen not to, or don't know how.

This issue is the key to raising your expectations for student behavior. And raising your expectations is the key to successful classroom behavior management.

Here's what we mean:

Can't vs. Won't

"*Can't* behave" means that a child's behavior cannot be influenced by you, or even by the child himself. Very few children *cannot* control their own behavior. Those who can't usually have organic or physical problems such as diagnosed hyperactivity.

"*Won't* behave" means that a child, for whatever reason, is choosing to behave inappropriately.

To illustrate this point, let's look at two situations you've probably experienced:

Situation #1—A Stranger Enters the Classroom

Each year in our school consultations we are called upon to observe hundreds of children with serious behavior problems. We've noticed something interesting in these observations. When we encounter these children for the first time, we rarely observe many who engage in inappropriate behavior.

Why is this so?

When a stranger enters a classroom, students don't know what to expect, and disruptions normally stop. Not knowing who the stranger is, or how he or she might respond to disruptive behavior, students *choose* to behave.

Do you see the point we're making? These students, though normally disruptive, clearly demonstrated to us and to their teachers that they can behave appropriately when they choose to.

If students choose to behave in one situation, surely they can be influenced to behave in other situations.

Let's look at another example:

Situation #2—State Testing Day

As we visit schools around the country, we're always struck by how well students behave on state testing day. We feel this is more than a coincidence. We have found that on state testing day teachers actually have higher expectations of their students. On state testing day, they know their students *can* (and *will*) behave and do as they are asked.

On state testing day teachers have an important agenda to meet, and they have no doubt that they will meet it. Through their words and actions, teachers communicate to their students, "It doesn't matter what kind of problems you have, how you've behaved throughout the year, today you will take the test, stay in your seat, and follow directions."

The teacher takes a direct, firm leadership position. There is no question on the part of the students what is expected of them and that the teacher will accept no excuses for misbehavior.

Can't vs. won't. It's an important distinction. If you feel that a student really *can't* behave, or that you can't influence him to behave, there is little or nothing you will be able to do to change his behavior. In essence, you've accepted defeat, so why bother communicating behavioral expectations to these students? Why bother setting limits for these kids? Why bother with positive reinforcement or consistent consequences? Why implement any of these behavior management techniques? They won't do any good anyway.

If, on the other hand, you recognize that some students *won't* behave, are choosing not to behave, or may not know how to behave, you are now empowered with both a purpose and a responsibility. Your road is clear: Your students *can* behave. It's up to you to determine a method to motivate them to choose a course of responsible behavior.

Once you accept that the vast majority of your students can behave, your expectations will be raised. And with expectations raised you are in a position to learn and implement the skills and techniques found in this book.

In the remainder of this text we will share with you how you can increase your ability to motivate students to manage their behavior in the classroom.

CHAPTER TWO — KEY POINTS

Roadblocks to Being Assertive

- A teacher's negative expectations about his or her ability to deal with disruptive student behavior is a major roadblock to successful classroom behavior management.

- Most students *can* behave. Those students who do not behave either choose not to, or haven't been taught.

- When a teacher believes that students *can* choose to behave, his or her expectations are raised.

- Positive expectations are key to successful classroom behavior management.

CHAPTER THREE

RESPONSE STYLES

Most teachers go into the classroom with the best of intentions. Few teachers want to intimidate students, turn them off, leave them unmotivated or lower their self-esteem. Teachers want success for their students.

But even the best-intentioned teacher sometimes responds to students in ways that sabotage classroom management efforts.

It is your response style that sets the tone of your classroom. It is your response style that impacts students' self-esteem and their success in school.

Here then is where we begin the process of increasing your ability to get your needs met and help students succeed in the classroom. It's important now to take a close look at how you respond to student behavior. This self-examination will help you recognize that some of your responses are effective, and some are not.

Through our years of working with educators, and of watching them interact with students in all kinds of situations, we have identified three types of responses that teachers consistently use in dealing with student behavior.

Two of these response styles are reactive in nature. That is, the teacher simply reacts to students' disruptive behavior. We call these response styles *nonassertive* and *hostile*.

The third, more effective response style, is proactive and reflects a teacher's commitment to teaching students to choose appropriate, responsible behavior. We call this the *assertive* response style.

Let's take a closer look now at each response style.

Nonassertive Response Style

A nonassertive response style is one in which the teacher is passive in responding to student behavior. He never clearly communicates his expectations to students ("Now please try to be good.") nor does he provide firm leadership. Instead, he simply reacts to the disruptive behavior of students as it appears and consequently feels as though he is constantly putting out fires.

A teacher who is basically nonassertive will be wishy-washy with students and very inconsistent in how he responds to behavior. One day he may allow students to disrupt without responding to them at all. The next day he may react firmly, demanding angrily that the students stop the same misbehavior.

Nonassertive responses leave students confused because they rarely know what to expect.

When a teacher responds nonassertively to students, he communicates that he is unsure of himself and his abilities. He appears powerless. This response style often results in a classroom environment in which there is constant testing of wills between the "powerless" teacher and the students.

Hostile Response Style

A teacher who responds in a hostile manner is one who may be able to get her needs to teach met in the classroom, but who does so at the expense of the feelings and self-esteem of her students. When a teacher responds in a hostile manner, she sends the message to students that "I don't like you," or "There is something wrong with you." Often teachers respond with hostility because they feel the only way to get students to behave is with rigid, authoritarian, "iron-fisted" discipline. These teachers will use discipline to control students rather than to teach them how to behave in a positive manner.

Hostile teachers sometimes describe the classroom as a battleground—them against the students. They often use discipline to get back at students rather than help them learn to behave more appropriately. Such teachers also have negative expectations of their ability to deal with students. They blame the students, the parents, and the administration for their problems.

Assertive Response Style

An assertive response style is one in which the teacher clearly, confidently and consistently states his expectations to students, and is prepared to back up these words with actions. When a teacher responds assertively, he tells students exactly what behavior is acceptable and what is unacceptable, what will happen when the student chooses to behave and what will happen when the student chooses not to behave. No questions. No room for confusion.

An assertive teacher has positive expectations of her ability to motivate students and a positive attitude is reflected in her words and actions. She is aware of her students' needs for limits and is prepared to set those limits. At the same time, she is cognizant of each student's need for warmth and encouragement and does not allow any student's appropriate behavior to go unrecognized.

Recognizing the realities of teaching in the 90s, the assertive teacher puts in the time and effort to systematically teach students how to behave.

> **Note:** No teacher responds nonassertively, in a hostile manner or assertively all the time, in all situations. On a good day, when you are feeling confident, you may respond more assertively. On a bad day, you may find more nonassertive or hostile responses creeping into your interactions with students. It is our goal to help you better understand the differences between the response styles so that when you find yourself responding in a nonassertive or hostile manner, you will be able to shift into a more assertive, positive approach to communicating with your students.

Now let's look at five typical classroom situations, and examine a nonassertive response, a hostile response and an assertive response to each.

Situation #1

A third-grade teacher directs her class to line up for recess. Three of the boys immediately leap from their desks and race to the door, pushing and shoving each other to be first in line.

● Nonassertive Response

The teacher pleads across the classroom, "Boys, how many times do I have to ask you to walk in the classroom? Now I'm tired of having to repeat myself. Next time will you please try and remember to act like third-graders?"

> Asking questions to which there is no logical response is a common nonassertive response. Nothing is conveyed to the student that could help him choose more responsible behavior. Likewise, some teachers feel so overwhelmed they end up pleading or begging. This timid approach is unlikely to communicate anything to students other than the fact that the teacher is powerless to effect any change.

● Hostile Response

The teacher harshly responds, "I've had it with you boys. I'll see all of you after school."

> Providing a consequence may in fact be appropriate, but the teacher's angry tone and words demean the students, and diminish their self-esteem.

● Assertive Response

The teacher calmly walks over to the door and speaks firmly and quietly to the three boys. "Kevin, Ryan, Steve, the rule is no running in the classroom. Now I want the three of you to stand at the end of the line–quietly and quickly."

This response sends a direct, clear message of the behavior the teacher expects.

Situation #2

A seventh-grade teacher is standing in front of the class giving a lecture. As he speaks, he notices that a few of the students in the back of the room are looking out the window or doodling. They aren't bothering anyone, but they are not paying any attention to what he is saying either.

- Nonassertive Response

The teacher simply ignores the students and continues his lecture. He thinks to himself, "There's nothing I can do about these students anyway."

> This teacher has negative expectations about his ability to keep all students on task and involved, so he gives up and does nothing at all, even though this is not in the best interest of his students. His response in effect gives students the message that their behavior is condoned.

- Hostile Response

Upon noticing the off-task behavior, the teacher stops the lesson cold and in a negative tone speaks to the students. "You kids in the back, I'm not standing up here just to hear myself talk. Wake up and pay attention. If you like staring out the window so much, I'll have you stay in after class and you can stare out the window all you want."

> Whether students are off task or not, they should never be treated in this abusive manner. This teacher may get the students to pay attention, but he does so at the expense of their dignity.

- Assertive Response

While continuing to lecture, the teacher walks to the back of the room and stands near those students who are off task. He doesn't stop his lesson for a moment, the other students don't break their concentration, and his close presence nudges the off-task students back on task.

> The assertive teacher firmly lets students know that they are expected to get back on task, but he does so in a way that enables him to teach and others to learn. His caring approach builds student self-esteem rather than reduces it.

Situation #3

In a ninth-grade classroom there is a student who is quite immature for his age and has a great deal of difficulty staying on task and not bothering other students. One day, while the class is divided into small learning groups, his teacher notices that he is participating in his group, staying on task and contributing to the assignment.

- Nonassertive Response

The teacher thinks to herself, "That's the first time he has worked this well with his group. That's real progress for him!" She does not, however, communicate her recognition or support to the student.

> Nonassertive teachers typically ignore students who are behaving appropriately. In so doing they lose the opportunity to positively reinforce and motivate those students, and at the same time they lose the opportunity to set a positive example for all students.

- Hostile Response

The teacher walks over to the student's group and states, "It's about time you're finally working like a ninth-grader should."

> This sarcastic response will only serve to embarrass the student. The result? An opportunity to build self-esteem is missed and the student is less likely to ever repeat the improved behavior.

- ## Assertive Response

The teacher catches the student's eye from across the room, smiles, and gives a nod of recognition. Later, as the class is being dismissed, she quietly speaks to the student: "You did a wonderful job working with your group today. Your contribution really helped everyone finish the assignment on time."

> This teacher's specific praise lets the student know that she really did notice and appreciate his good efforts in class. Likewise, her sensitivity in not singling him out about his behavior in front of his peers speaks volumes about her caring approach to behavior management.

Situation #4

It's the beginning of the school year. The teacher gives her students directions to line up for recess. The students follow the directions quickly, quietly and appropriately.

- ## Nonassertive Response

The nonassertive teacher watches the students as they line up and says nothing. She thinks to herself, "Good, at least I don't have to deal with any problems."

> The nonassertive teacher just takes it for granted that students know how to behave. Because of this, she doesn't feel or understand the need for positively reinforcing their appropriate behavior.

- ## Hostile Response

The teacher sees his students complying with the directions and says, "It's about time today that you kids did something you were told to."

> This sarcastic response will in no way motivate students to keep up their good effort.

- ## Assertive Response

The teacher watches as the students follow her directions. Smiling, she comments, "Bob's lining up quietly. Andrea and Cynthia are too. Seth, thank you for putting your books away and lining up so quickly."

> The assertive teacher goes out of her way to recognize her students' appropriate behavior. She doesn't take their behavior for granted. Instead, she makes a point of recognizing the good behavior as it appears. She knows that her reinforcement will increase the likelihood of students repeating the good effort.

Situation #5

In a sixth-grade class there is a belligerent student who is provoking other students around him. The teacher tells him to stop bothering his classmates and get to work. The student responds, "I don't want to do any of this stupid work."

- ## Nonassertive Response

The teacher throws up his hands and says to the student, "What's wrong with you? If you don't get to work and stop bothering other students, you're going to detention." The student giggles and quietly continues his disruptive behavior. The teacher just walks away. As the student expects, the teacher gives no consequence at all.

> Students quickly learn that empty threats of punishment are easily ignored.

- ## Hostile Response

This teacher moves over to the student and yells into his face: "That's it. You've got a lousy attitude and I've had it with you. One more word out of you and I'm kicking you out of this class."

> At being confronted in this manner in front of his peers, the student seethes in anger. He responds, "That's fine with me," and storms out of the room, slamming the door as he leaves. In spite of his earlier bravado, his humiliation is obvious.

This angry confrontation only serves to escalate the situation. Nobody wins, and the teacher and student are more alienated than ever.

- Assertive Response

The teacher calmly gives the student a consequence from his classroom discipline plan. "Jeff, that's one minute after class." Jeffrey responds, "Big deal, I don't care."

At this response, the teacher walks over to Jeffrey and calmly says, "Let's go outside and talk." Outside the classroom he says, "Jeff, you have a choice. You can either settle down and get to work now or you can go to the office with me and call your mother. I cannot allow you to act this way in class."

The teacher de-escalates this situation in a calm, firm manner. By removing Jeff from the classroom, and getting him away from his peers, he removes his audience and has his complete attention. His response leaves no doubt in the student's mind what the teacher wants him to do. The teacher follows through calmly with the consequences from his discipline plan, and through his words and attitude lets the student know that he is serious.

Effects of Nonassertive, Hostile and Assertive Response Styles

As we have stated, most teachers fall into all three response styles at one time or another.

The purpose of this chapter is to increase your awareness of these response styles so that you can better avoid nonassertive and hostile responses, while at the same time increase your assertive responses.

But what happens when a teacher finds herself responding nonassertively most of the time? What happens when a hostile response seems to be all a teacher can give?

It's important to understand the overall effect that inappropriate responses can have on both teacher and students. It's important to understand that developing an assertive response style is basic to successful classroom management.

Nonassertive

A nonassertive teacher will feel frustrated and inadequate due to his inability to get his needs met in the classroom. The stress he experiences will eventually result in his becoming "burned out" and fed up both with students and his profession.

The nonassertive teacher may also feel a good deal of inner hostility toward the students he feels he cannot handle. This hostility may not be openly expressed to the student, or it may suddenly burst forth in a hostile response by the teacher. This pent-up hostility is a serious block to the development of a positive student-teacher relationship.

The students of a nonassertive teacher often feel frustrated, manipulated and angry.

These students do not receive the clear limits they need to function successfully in the classroom. One day the teacher may mean what he says, the next three days he doesn't. The students may have to sit through barrages of threats without knowing whether the threats are real or meaningless. Students resent these situations and many will try to get away with all they can. They will test the teacher continually to see if he does or doesn't mean what he says that day. The students will learn to con the teacher in order to manipulate him around those limits that are set. The inevitable testing by the students results in a chaotic environment of constant disruption that damages students educationally and emotionally.

When a teacher is nonassertive, students learn also that their appropriate behavior is generally unnoticed, thus there is little motivation to behave appropriately. Or, if a nonassertive teacher does try to give praise or rewards, it is often inappropriate to the grade level or perceived as a form of bribery. In such a situation, a student might say, "What will we get if we do the homework?"

In general, students have little or no respect for a nonassertive teacher. If most of a teacher's responses to students are nonassertive, she will have little success in motivating them to behave appropriately.

Hostile

Contrary to the belief of many students, few teachers like to be mean and hostile. The hostile teacher exercises a negative stance because she feels it is the only way she can maintain control. This teacher is afraid to let go of her iron grip because she feels it is the only way she can get the students to do what she wants. She doesn't like being the way she is, and thus may feel guilty about how she deals with students. The fear, guilt and negative responses become major stumbling blocks to the development of anything but negative, self-defeating teacher-student relationships.

Students quickly learn to fear and dislike hostile teachers. The teacher often becomes the enemy. Students do what they can—lie, cheat, or feign illness—to get around the perceived unfair negative limits of the teacher.

The often unexpressed hostility students feel toward the teacher can end up being transferred to their classmates. After a morning of being berated and belittled, students not only feel put down, but also angry. It would not be unusual to witness a good deal of teasing, poking and fighting among students as they try to release the frustrations built up from the morning in the classroom.

Many students do what is asked of them in a hostile teacher's classroom, but they behave out of anxiety or fear.

As a result, they learn not only to dislike the teacher, but school as well. The negative atmosphere wears away at the self-image and self-esteem of the students. After such a negative day at school, even a student with a healthy sense of self-esteem becomes less motivated. A student who already has a low self concept becomes a more likely "drop out" candidate. These feelings come home with the student and often can result in the parent disliking the school as well.

Assertive

A teacher who responds assertively to students creates an atmosphere in which both she and the students have an opportunity to get their needs met. The atmosphere is positive with a balance established between the rights of the students and the rights of the teacher, and between firm limits and warmth and support.

The assertive teacher takes the responsibility for getting her needs met in the classroom. By fulfilling her needs, she is more capable of meeting the needs of students and thus reaping the internal and external benefits one gets from performing well professionally.

This does not mean that an assertive teacher's behavior management results in a perfect classroom where all is sweetness and light, where all students learn and behave to their full potential, or where she never has a rough day with the students. What it does mean is that the assertive teacher has the satisfaction of knowing she has accepted her professional responsibility and has done everything in her power to do the best job she is capable of doing.

The assertive teacher usually feels accomplished and good about herself at the end of the day.

Students learn to trust and respect an assertive teacher. They know that this teacher means what she says, and says what she means. They clearly know the boundaries of acceptable and unacceptable behavior. Thus, they have the opportunity to choose how they want to behave while knowing fully what the consequences will be for their misbehavior. As one student put it: "He is a fair teacher. If you're good, he'll let you know he likes it. And if you mess up, he won't let you get away with it. You know he's there with you all the time. It really feels kind of neat."

An assertive teacher tries to establish an atmosphere where she maximizes the potential for developing a positive teacher-student relationship between herself and each and every student.

> **Begin now to listen to your own responses** to student behavior in your classroom. If you hear yourself responding nonassertively or with hostility, make a mental note to remember the situation that generated the ineffective response. As you continue reading this text, you will be given the skills to respond assertively and effectively to most classroom situations.

As you will discover in the remainder of this book, an assertive response style is an integral part of becoming an assertive teacher.

CHAPTER THREE — KEY POINTS

Response Styles

- The manner in which you respond to student behavior impacts students' self-esteem and students' success in school.

- We have identified three basic response styles: nonassertive, hostile and assertive.

- A nonassertive response style is one in which the teacher is passive and inconsistent in responding to student behavior. This teacher often simply reacts to disruptive behavior as it appears, rather than proactively plan for it.

- The students of a nonassertive teacher often feel frustrated, manipulated and angry. They do not receive the clear limits they need to function successfully in the classroom.

- A hostile response style is one in which the teacher responds to students in a hostile, rigid, authoritarian manner, often at the expense of students' feelings and self-esteem.

- The hostile teacher is perceived as unfair, and students behave out of anxiety and fear rather than through making responsible behavior choices.

- An assertive response style is one in which the teacher clearly, confidently and consistently states expectations to students and is prepared to back up these words with actions.

- Students learn to trust and respect an assertive teacher because they clearly know the parameters that have been set for acceptable and unacceptable behavior.

YOUR CLASSROOM DISCIPLINE PLAN

YOUR CLASSROOM DISCIPLINE PLAN

It's time to move on now to developing the practical skills you need for successful behavior management in your classroom. The focus of this section is understanding and developing your classroom discipline plan.

Developing and using this plan are the most important, preventive actions you can take in managing the behavior of your students—and in teaching them to choose responsible behavior.

In Chapter 4 we will introduce you to the classroom discipline plan. Then, in Chapters 5, 6 and 7, we are going to take you through the steps of developing a discipline plan for your own classroom. The goal is for you to create a plan that is tailor-made for meeting your needs and the needs of your students.

In Chapter 8, we will give you guidelines for developing lessons to teach your students your classroom discipline plan.

CHAPTER FOUR

WHAT IS A CLASSROOM DISCIPLINE PLAN?

A classroom discipline plan is a system that allows you to clarify the behaviors you expect from students and what they can expect from you in return. The goal of a classroom discipline plan is to have a fair and consistent way to establish a safe, orderly, positive classroom environment in which you can teach and students can learn.

Your classroom discipline plan will allow you to integrate effective behavior management into your teaching routine—whatever your grade level, whatever your style of teaching. It is a dynamic, flexible system that recognizes your individual needs as a teacher, and the needs of your particular students. Above all, a classroom discipline plan stresses positive recognition as the most powerful tool at your disposal for encouraging responsible behavior and raising student self-esteem.

The plan consists of three parts:

- **RULES** that students must follow at all times.

- **POSITIVE RECOGNITION** that students will receive for following the rules.

- **CONSEQUENCES** that result when students choose not to follow the rules.

Here are two sample discipline plans. In Chapters 5, 6 and 7 we will look closely at how to choose rules, positive recognition and consequences for your own classroom.

Sample Discipline Plan for Elementary Students

Classroom Rules

Follow directions.

Keep hands, feet, objects to yourself.

No teasing or name calling.

Positive Recognition

Praise

First in line for recess

Positive notes sent home to parents

Positive notes to students

Eat lunch with teacher

Select own seat on Friday

Consequences

First time a student breaks a rule:	Warning
Second time:	Last in line for recess or lunch
Third time:	10 minutes away from group
Fourth time:	Teacher calls parents
Fifth time:	Send to principal
Severe Clause:	Send to principal

Sample Discipline Plan for Secondary Students

Classroom Rules

Follow directions.

Be in the classroom and seated when the bell rings.

Do not swear.

Positive Recognition

Praise

Positive notes sent home to parents

Privilege pass

Consequences

First time a student breaks a rule:	Warning
Second time:	Stay in class 1 minute after the bell
Third time:	Stay in class 2 minutes after the bell
Fourth time:	Call parents
Fifth time:	Send to principal

Severe Clause: Send to principal

What will your classroom discipline plan do for you and your students?

Why establish a classroom discipline plan? Let's take a look at some of the benefits.

A discipline plan makes managing student behavior much easier.

Without a clear plan for responding to student behavior, you are forced to constantly make choices about how to react to student behavior. These on-the-spot responses are likely to be arbitrary, inconsistent and emotional.

A classroom discipline plan helps you respond quickly, assertively and with confidence to student behavior. Without a plan, teachers often suffer through students' misbehavior until their resistance collapses and they explode in rage.

A discipline plan protects students' rights.

A discipline plan helps ensure that you deal with each student in a fair and consistent manner. Teachers who do not have a plan tend to *react* to students, and many times their consequences are not fair.

Here's a prime example of what we often see:

> Early in the day, Kyle talked out in class, disrupting the lesson in progress. His teacher gave him a warning and continued with her lesson. Later that same day, Jamie also talked out, interrupting a student who was presenting an oral report. The teacher, visibly annoyed, disciplined Jamie by taking away recess. Finally, at the end of the day, when the teacher was tired and her temper a bit frayed, Bradley talked out. This time the teacher lost her temper, yelled at Bradley and called his parents that night about his problem behavior.

This wasn't fair or consistent. All students have the right to be treated fairly and equally. All students have the right to the same due process in the classroom. Students need to know that when a rule is broken, they will receive a specific consequence. Everybody wants to be treated equally. When your students can rely on equal treatment, they will accept your rules and directions more readily.

A discipline plan helps ensure parental support.

As we'll discuss in detail later, you need parental support. You need to know that you can call upon parents to support your academic, behavioral and homework efforts. Before giving that support, however, parents will want to know that you are genuinely concerned about their child.

Communicating your classroom discipline plan to parents shows them that you care about teaching their children how to behave responsibly. It also demonstrates your own professionalism and confidence in your ability to manage the classroom.

A discipline plan helps ensure administrator support.

A discipline plan demonstrates to your administrator that you have a well thought-out blueprint for managing student behavior in your classroom. A discipline plan shows that you are in control and that you will not simply send a student to the office whenever there is a problem. When your administrator understands the commitment you've made to effective classroom management, you will be better able to get support when you need it.

Guidelines for introducing your discipline plan to parents and to your administrator are given in Chapter 17.

CHAPTER FOUR — KEY POINTS

What Is a Classroom Discipline Plan?

- A classroom discipline plan consists of three parts:

  1. **Rules** that students must follow at all times.

  2. **Positive recognition** that students will receive for following the rules.

  3. **Consequences** that result when students choose not to follow the rules.

- A discipline plan makes managing student behavior much easier.

- A discipline plan protects students' rights.

- A discipline plan helps ensure parental support.

- A discipline plan helps ensure administrator support.

CHAPTER FIVE

CREATING YOUR CLASSROOM DISCIPLINE PLAN

Part 1: Rules

Each year brings new students to your classroom. They come with their own needs, their own past experiences and their own expectations. They come with their preconceptions of who you are, what your limits will be, how they will relate to you, and you to them.

They want to know: What expectations do you have for us?

Unless *you* know how you want your students to behave, how will *they* know?

To successfully manage your classroom, you first have to know how you want your students to behave. You need to be very clear about what your expectations are, and how you will communicate those expectations. As one master teacher we worked with told us:

> "Increasing numbers of students are coming to school from homes where expectations are undefined and rules are either unstated or unenforced. Young people need the structure and guidance that appropriate classroom expectations and rules provide. Today more than ever, behavioral expectations carry with them an importance beyond the classroom. They help teach what the student may not be getting anywhere else—responsible behavior. When students learn to behave responsibly, their self-esteem rises and their motivation to achieve increases."

As you begin to formulate your classroom rules, ask yourself, "What general behaviors do I need at all times, day in and day out, so that I can teach and my students can learn? What expectations do I have for how students conduct themselves in my classroom?"

We have found that successful teachers have a minimal number of rules which are in effect at all times, in all activities, all day long.

Here are some rules that teachers typically need in order to teach, in order for students to learn, and in order to have a positive classroom environment.

- **Follow directions.**

   This is perhaps the most important rule you will establish. You can't teach and students won't learn if the many directions you give throughout the day aren't followed.

- **Keep hands, feet and objects to yourself.**

   For students to have a safe and orderly classroom, they need to know that they are protected from being hit, kicked, or their property being taken or destroyed.

- **No profanity or teasing.**

   All children have the right to be in a classroom where they will not be verbally or psychologically humiliated.

These basic rules are common to most successful teachers' classrooms. Other appropriate general expectations that teachers have established include:

- No eating.

- Be in your seat when the bell rings.

- Walk in the classroom.

- Do not leave the classroom without permission.

- No yelling or screaming.

What do all of these basic rules have in common? What makes them appropriate general classroom rules?

First, these rules are observable. They address behaviors that teachers can clearly see. The more observable a rule is, the easier it is for students to understand and comply with it. Rules such as "be nice" and "treat each other kindly," while important goals, are not behaviors that can be readily seen. Such vague expectations may mean one thing to one child, and an entirely different thing to another. Thus, the rules cannot be readily enforced. Remember, the clearer your expectations, the easier they are for students to follow.

Observable Rules	Vague Expectations
• Keep hands to yourself.	• Show respect to other students.
• Be in your seat when the bell rings.	• No fooling around.
• No yelling or screaming.	• No unnecessary talking.

Second, each of these rules is applicable throughout the entire day. No exceptions. They apply no matter what activity is taking place. Many times we have seen teachers establish general rules for the classroom that are not enforceable throughout the school day or class period. Because they really aren't in effect at all times, these rules can cause more problems than they prevent, and actually, through their ambiguity, hinder the teacher's ability to teach students to behave.

With these guidelines in mind, you can understand why you would avoid using rules such as these:

- Raise your hand and wait to be called upon before you speak.

  Though this rule sounds sensible, it is not enforceable all day long. There are going to be many times during the school day when students will be expected to speak out—for example, in cooperative learning groups, or during transitions. Realistically, there will be times each day when you will not expect students to raise their hands before speaking. Because of these exceptions, we have found that this is confusing as a general classroom rule.

- Stay in your seat unless you have permission to get up.

  Always? Can a student ever get up to get a sheet of paper? Ever sharpen a pencil? Again, if the rule is not 100% enforceable throughout the day, it is not an appropriate general classroom rule.

- Use a 12-inch voice in the classroom.

  Of course there are many times during the day when you will want your students to speak in a soft voice that can't be heard beyond a foot away. But there are also times when students need to speak up. Again, too many exceptions render this rule unenforceable all day or all period.

- Complete all homework assignments.

  This rule sounds all right. Obviously you need students to complete homework. But the problem with a rule like this is that it does not relate to classroom behavior. There may be times when the student does not understand the assignment. There may be times when completing an assignment is out of his or her control. This rule belongs in a separate homework policy.

Remember, classroom rules must be designed to teach appropriate classroom behavior.

When you establish general classroom rules that do not clearly reflect your consistent expectations you run the risk of confusing students. In truth, you will not be able to enforce these rules with any meaningful consistency. There will always be an element of doubt as to when one of these rules is in force or not. You probably won't be sure, and neither will your students.

Now let's look at some appropriate general classroom rules for different grade levels:

Grades K-3

- Follow directions.

- Keep hands, feet and objects to yourself.

- Do not leave the room without permission.

- No swearing or teasing.

- No yelling or screaming.

Grades 4-6

- Follow directions.

- Keep hands, feet and objects to yourself.

- No swearing or teasing.

- No yelling or screaming.

Grades 7-12

- Follow directions.

- No swearing or teasing.

- Be in your seat when the bell rings.

Notice that each and every one of the rules listed is observable and each one is a behavioral expectation that can be in effect at all times.

Choose the rules that work for you.

When you develop your own general classroom rules, ask yourself this important question: Do I want students to comply with this rule at all times? It's important that the expectations you have for your own classroom fit your needs and the needs of your students. Copying someone else's rules, or ones from this book, will not guarantee that your rules will be effective for you.

Ask students for their suggestions.

Many teachers also find it helpful to involve students in choosing some of the rules for the classroom. Ask students these questions: "How do other students stop you from learning?" "What rules would make it easier for you to learn?"

Keep in mind that many times students' rules are more strict than those determined by teachers. Therefore, you should have a clear idea of the rules you would like to include before opening a discussion with your students. As the discussion progresses, guide the students so that their suggested rules are both appropriate and realistic. Consider student input, but be sure that the final rules you choose follow the guidelines in this chapter, and your own needs as the teacher.

By including students in your selection of rules you will give them ownership in the classroom discipline plan. They will see the rules as their rules and will be motivated to support and remind each other about following the rules.

In Chapter 6 we will take a look at how positive recognition will motivate students to follow your rules and choose responsible behavior.

CHAPTER FIVE — KEY POINTS

Rules

- Choose classroom rules that will let students know what behaviors are expected in the classroom at all times.

- Choose a limited number of rules.

- Choose rules that are observable. Vague rules are difficult to comply with and difficult to enforce.

- Choose rules that can apply at all times throughout the day or period.

- Choose rules that apply to behavior only. Rules for a classroom discipline plan must not address academic or homework issues.

- Consider involving students in choosing some of the rules for your classroom.

CREATING YOUR CLASSROOM DISCIPLINE PLAN

Part 2: Positive Recognition

Today you must come to class prepared not only to teach subject matter, but to motivate students to behave appropriately as well.

We've already discussed the changes today's students are facing. Topping that list is an increasing lack of student motivation to learn or to behave appropriately. Without a teacher's committed efforts to motivate them, many students will never achieve their potential, others will flounder through school, and still others will ultimately drop out.

Positive recognition is your key to motivating students to succeed:

- Positive recognition motivates students to choose appropriate behavior and creates a positive atmosphere in the classroom.

- Positive recognition is the sincere and meaningful attention you give a student for behaving according to your expectations.

- Positive recognition, as you will see, must become the most active part of your classroom discipline plan.

What will positive recognition do for your classroom?

Positive recognition will:

- Encourage students to continue appropriate behavior.

- Increase students' self-esteem.

- Dramatically reduce problem behaviors.

- Create a positive classroom environment for you and your students.

- Help you teach appropriate behavior and establish positive relationships with students.

Let's look more closely.

Positive recognition encourages students to continue appropriate behavior.

When teachers recognize appropriate behavior, they provide students positive reinforcement for their actions. Thus, the students are more likely to continue their appropriate behavior in order to receive the recognition they need.

Positive recognition reinforces those students who usually behave with a well-deserved pat on the back while, at the same time, prompting those students with behavior problems to change their behavior.

When you like the way a student is doing something, let him know—he just might do it again!

Positive recognition increases a student's self-esteem.

Everyone likes to be praised. Everyone likes positive recognition. If the majority of your responses are negative, it tears down the self-esteem of your students.

Motivate your students. When self-esteem is low, classroom troubles are higher.

Positive recognition reduces problem behaviors.

Who gets the most attention in classrooms, the disruptive student or the well-behaved student? We all know that it's easy to ignore the "good" child while expending energy on the student who's causing problems. Effective use of positive recognition turns this situation around.

As a teacher, you know students are going to vie for your attention one way or another. Assure them that they'll receive your attention when they do their work and when they behave appropriately. If you don't praise students for being good—if they don't receive the attention they need for behaving appropriately—they'll continue to vie for your attention in other ways.

By responding positively to appropriate behavior, you quickly teach your students that they can get the attention they want, need and deserve by behaving. When students learn that you will give them attention for positive behavior, they will choose to act in a positive way rather than in a negative manner. Your class will begin to run on some of its own positive momentum.

Consistent positive recognition helps improve relationships with students.

Think about it. Who wants a school day filled with negativity and tension? Yet that's what many teachers have.

If you feel that the only way you can "make students behave" is to reprimand or punish them, chances are your days are filled with tension. You're probably frustrated and so are your students. Overuse of negative consequences will create a classroom environment that pulls teacher and student apart.

The overuse of negative consequences, and the underuse of positive recognition, is a major flaw in many classroom management efforts.

Provide positive recognition—frequently, and then some!

The more consistently you use praise and positive recognition to influence students, the better your students will feel about you, the better you will feel about yourself and the more motivated the class will be to achieve your academic and social goals.

But if positive recognition is so good for us, why are we so negative?

Now that we've looked at the benefits of positive recognition, consider these questions:

- Do you consistently recognize and reinforce students who follow the rules of the classroom?

- Do you make it a point to always be on the lookout for appropriate behavior? Is "Catch them being good" one of your most important goals each day?

If you can't answer with a resounding yes, you're not alone.

Why don't most teachers use more positive recognition? If positive recognition is so powerful, if hundreds of studies and articles drive this point home, if every book on the subject of classroom management confirms it, if in every workshop on behavior you hear "Be more positive," why then do most teachers fail to implement it to its fullest advantage? Why do we drop the ball and, in many cases, forget about positive recognition completely?

Is it that we really don't care about kids? **Nonsense!**

The truth is, under the stress and strain of the classroom, educators tend to <u>react</u> negatively to pressure.

Our classroom observations have consistently shown us that approximately 90% of teachers' comments to students regarding behavior are negative. When we all know how beneficial positive recognition is for students, why do we fall so easily into focusing on the negative and overlooking the positive?

It's not that we want to be negative. On the contrary, there are sound physiological reasons why we respond so consistently to negative behavior rather than positive behavior. Here's what we mean:

Picture an anxiety-level scale of 0 to 100.

At 0 your anxiety is so low you're probably asleep. At 100 you are having a panic attack. In normal situations, let's say your anxiety level in the classroom is at 50. What happens to your anxiety level if a student loudly disrupts or refuses to do what you've asked? Your anxiety level will probably rise sharply.

Why?

What is the biggest underlying fear educators have? *The entire class getting out of control.* Simply imagining this can send one's anxiety level skyrocketing. When our anxiety level rises, we respond physiologically. The brain tells us there is a threat and that something must be done immediately to lower the anxiety that is causing so much discomfort. Thus, you might abruptly tell the student to be quiet and provide a disciplinary consequence in an attempt to quickly lower the anxiety level.

On the other hand, how do you physiologically respond when students are well-behaved? Your anxiety level may drop, but at a very slow rate. There is no voice in your head telling you to do something immediately. No panic. No sense of urgency.

Now, given our natural tendency to react strongly to disruptive behavior, what can you do to circumvent these reactions? How can you keep from falling into the trap of negativity?

Plan to be positive.

How does one plan to be positive each day? Look to your classroom discipline plan.

Your classroom discipline plan is a dynamic system that gives you a natural foundation for being positive every day in class.

Every day students are expected to follow rules. When they follow those rules, recognize them! As part of your classroom management planning, you should decide ahead of time which positives you will use. This means having a variety of reinforcers to use for individual students and reinforcers you can use on a classwide basis.

First, let's take a look at how to provide positive recognition to individual students.

Individual Positive Recognition

Individual positive reinforcers include:

- Praise

- Positive notes and phone calls home

- Special privileges

- Behavior awards

- Tangible rewards

Praise: The Most Powerful Positive Support You Can Give

What's the easiest way to motivate students? Praise. The most effective? Praise. What positive recognition can you give to your students at any time? Under all circumstances? Praise.

You can praise a student anytime, anywhere.

Praise is the most meaningful, effective positive recognition you can give. When you take the time to verbally recognize a student's achievement, you are making a powerful statement. You are saying, "I care about you. I notice the good work you are doing and I'm proud of you."

The single most important attribute we've found that distinguishes successful classroom managers from less effective ones is that they praise their students frequently.

It isn't by accident, either. They make a conscious decision—"I will recognize good behavior. I will look for the positive behavior in kids, and I will say something about it."

Praise should be your #1 choice for positively recognizing student behavior.

But there are other effective techniques you will also want to include in your classroom discipline plan as well.

Positive Notes and Phone Calls

Successful classroom management means that you have to reach out beyond your classroom.

Letting your students know that you will send positive notes to parents is a great motivator for students. That alone is reason enough for contacting parents with good news.

But just as important as reinforcing students is establishing a positive rapport with the parents of your students. Throughout the year you will need their support. Don't make the mistake of waiting until a problem arises to reach out to parents. Contact them with good news and it will be much easier to get their support when a problem arises.

Just think of the impact on the student, too. This positive contact says, "I not only care how you behave in my room, I want your parents to know as well."

It sounds good, but we know what probably comes to your mind first:

> "Phone calls and notes home? I'm busy. I have 80 other things to do."

> "Where would I fit phone calls into my day?"

> "Are they so important that I have to plan for them?"

They are that important and they do not have to be time consuming.

A positive phone call or note home is one of the most time-effective means of getting parents on your side—of letting them know that you care about their child and want to share their child's successes.

And what does it involve? **Just five minutes a day.**

Look at it this way: Each phone call will take about two minutes. Two calls a day, that's ten a week. In a month, an elementary teacher can make positive contact with each and every parent! And at this rate, a secondary teacher can speak to each parent during the semester.

Again, planning is everything. Those five minutes won't just appear in the morning or afternoon unless you schedule them. You have to make the time before you can take the time. So set it aside—five minutes with a phone. It can only help improve your teacher-parent relationships.

The results are tremendous in terms of increasing a student's self-esteem. When a student feels that his parents and his teacher are working with him, for him and together, that's motivation!

Here's what a positive phone call to a parent might sound like:

> "I want you to know that Sara is really setting a wonderful example for the other students. She follows my directions as soon as I give them, and that helps everybody get to work more easily and quickly."

> "I'm just so pleased that she's made such a great start. I feel confident that this is going to be a very good year for Sara."

> "Please tell Sara that I called and how pleased I am with her behavior in class."

And here's what a positive note might say:

September 28

Dear Mr. and Mrs. Dawson:

It's a pleasure to let you know what a terrific job Rick is doing in my class. Every day he arrives to class on time and settles down to work right away. I think you'll find that his responsible behavior will be resulting in better grades! You should be very proud of the effort he's making!

Sincerely,

Including parents in their children's successes is a sure way to send positive messages home, and bring some motivation back to class. Give that added support that will benefit your students. Take those important five minutes a day and turn them into a year-long advantage.

Set a goal for yourself to make a specific number of positive contacts each week. Remember, it's simple math.

Behavior Awards

Special awards for good behavior can be highly significant motivators for students of any age. Award certificates usually have a long-lasting effect because students proudly take them home and post them for the rest of the family to see. Parents report that awards often stay on the refrigerator door for months at a time.

Here again, plan to send home a specific number of behavior awards each week. Be particularly on the lookout for those students who have to work harder at controlling their behavior, and recognize the extra effort they are making.

Here are examples of behavior awards for younger students and for older students:

Keep a supply of behavior awards ready to use and you'll see just how effective, motivational and appreciated they can be.

Special Privileges

Allowing a student to take part in an activity he or she particularly enjoys is often a great motivator. Verbally reinforce the appropriate behavior when awarding the privilege: "Thank you for putting all the balls away after PE, Amy. That was very thoughtful of you."

Here are some suggestions for special privileges.

Elementary	Secondary
First in line	Extra computer time
Tutor younger children	Excused from one pop quiz
Class monitor job	Take one problem off a test
Read special book	First out of class
Work on favorite activity	Sit by a friend for one period
Correct papers	

Tangible Rewards

Most students will respond to praise, positive notes or special privileges. There may be, however, one or two students in your classroom who simply are not motivated by these positive reinforcers. You may have a student who comes from a home where positive recognition is never used. At first this student may be embarrassed by verbal praise and be uncomfortable receiving it. A tangible reward may hold more interest. It may be the only reinforcement perceived by the student as a positive.

It doesn't matter that the reward is a sticker or a trinket with little monetary value. What is important is that the student earns a reward that he or she can see and touch.

But pay heed. You must use tangible rewards sparingly or they will lose their effectiveness. Planned out and used properly, tangible rewards will be effective motivators for some students.

Tangible rewards are not bribery!

Some educators may feel that the use of tangible rewards such as treats, stickers or small trinkets is bribery. We do not believe this to be so.

Let's make a few points perfectly clear:

- A bribe is given in anticipation of a behavior.

- A reward is given as a result of a behavior.

- A bribe is given to entice someone to do something that they would not normally do because it is not in their best interest.

- A reward is given in recognition of a behavior that is in a student's best interest.

Finally, bribery is defined as giving an individual something of value to perform an unethical and illegal act. We do not believe that behaving in a positive manner is illegal or immoral. Some children simply need these rewards to get them on track.

The point is this: There are going to be times when tangible rewards are the only positives that will work—the only way you can motivate a student. Use them, but use them with care.

Follow these guidelines for using tangible rewards:

- Be sure to give the reward immediately after you have observed the desired behavior. You want the student to associate this behavior with the reward.

- Whenever you give a student a tangible reward, always pair it with praise such as, "Bobby, here's a sticker for sitting so quietly. I'm really proud of you."

Tangible rewards are particularly effective on days when students tend to be overly excited. Fridays and days before holidays or vacations can be particularly trying for even the most skilled teachers. In these situations you will find that tangible rewards are effective tools for keeping students on task.

Classwide Positive Recognition

In previous pages we've discussed how you can recognize individual students for their positive behavior.

Many teachers also find it beneficial to plan to recognize and reinforce classwide behavior. These teachers use what we call a classwide positive recognition system.

A classwide positive recognition system is a program in which all the students—not just one student—work towards a positive reward that will be given to the entire class. The goal of a classwide recognition system is to have a means to motivate students to learn a new behavior or to work on a problem behavior. It shows students how important it is to work together in a cooperative manner to achieve a common goal.

Here's an example of how a classwide system works:

Mrs. Crane teaches seventh grade. During the first week of school she has decided to use a classwide recognition system to help motivate her students to learn to follow directions quickly and appropriately. Here's how she presented the idea to the class:

> "One of the most important rules you need to learn in my class is to follow directions when I give them. During the past few days we've discussed how you should behave when I give directions for different activities. Now I have a great idea that will help you get into the habit of quickly following these directions whenever I give them. Here's what we'll do:

> "Every time I give a direction, I'll be looking for those of you who do what I ask. For example, if I say, 'Take out your math workbooks and begin the assignment,' I'll be looking for those of you who follow that direction. Then, when I catch you following the direction, I'm going to put a point here on the board for the entire class. You've told me that you really want to have free time. So when all of you—working together—have earned 50 points, you will earn the right to have 15 minutes of free time.

> "I'll bet all of you are so good at following directions we'll earn that 15 minutes by tomorrow. Any questions?

> "Good! Now, please take out your math books. Walter and Jennifer have their books out. That's a point for the class! Good work! Eddie and Barbara are ready, too. That's another point!"

The teacher marks points on the board as students comply.

Here are four points to keep in mind when considering a classroom recognition system:

- A powerful reason why a classwide recognition system works well is because it makes use of peer pressure. It's not uncommon for students to cooperatively remind each other, "Hey, listen to the teacher. If we get five more points, we get free time." This is especially true of middle school and secondary students.

- A classwide recognition system is particularly effective when working on a specific classwide problem behavior such as students noisily entering the classroom after lunch.

- To be effective, a classwide recognition system should be implemented as needed throughout the year. It is not meant to be in effect at all times. A classwide recognition system is designed to be used as a prescription for correcting a specific problem.

- Although many teachers find it helpful to develop models that motivate all students to work cooperatively toward a class reward, other teachers find that individual positive recognition works just as well in their classrooms. Use your professional judgment to determine this for your style of teaching.

Here's how to set up a classwide recognition system:

1. Pick a system you are comfortable with, and one that is appropriate to the age of your students. (See suggestions on pages 73-75.)

2. Choose a reward that you are comfortable giving, but make sure that whatever the class earns, it is something they will want to work toward. If you're unsure, just ask them! Student involvement can help increase interest in achieving the behavioral goals you set.

Here are some ideas for classwide rewards:

Elementary Classwide Rewards

- Special movie

- Extra free time in class

- Special arts and crafts project

- Extra PE time

- Invite a special visitor to class

Secondary Classwide Rewards

- Movie with popcorn

- Radio in class

- Coupons from student store

- 5 minutes of talk time in class

- Free reading time

- Free choice of seat for a day

---

3. Make sure the students earn the reward in a timely manner. Set a goal for how quickly you want the class to earn a reward. Then monitor the frequency with which you are awarding points to ensure that you and the students are on track. Be sure to set reasonable goals. Younger or more immature students should earn a reward in far less time than a secondary class.

Classwide Reward Time Goals

Grades K-1:   1 day

Grades 2-3:   2 days to 1 week

Grades 4-6:   1 week

Grades 7-12:   1 to 2 weeks

4. Once the class has earned points toward a classwide reward, do not take away points for misbehavior. Also, all students, regardless of negative consequences they may have earned individually, must participate in the classwide reward. If you impose a consequence and take away the classwide reward, you are providing two consequences for one misbehavior.

Suggested Classwide Recognition Systems

Once you decide to use a classwide recognition system, you'll need to have a way of keeping track of the points your students earn. Here are some examples of programs teachers find practical, effective and motivating.

Points on the Board

Designate a corner of your chalkboard to serve as the Classwide Reward Scoreboard. On the scoreboard write the number of points needed to reach the class reward. Then, when you see a student or group of students behaving appropriately, restate the appropriate behavior and put a mark on the board.

> "Paul, Sandy and Evan have followed directions and are getting out their science reports. That's a point for the class."

At the end of the day total up the points. Remind the class of their progress. Then at the beginning of class each day remind students of the score and the reward they are working toward.

> "You've earned 35 points so far this week. Just 15 points more and we'll have the popcorn party on Friday. Keep up the good work."

Marbles in a Jar

This system is easy to use and is very popular with younger students. The combination of brightly colored marbles and the sound they make as they are dropped into the jar is motivating in itself.

Here's how to use Marbles in a Jar:

- Place a plastic jar on your desk. Tell your students that when they follow your rules, you will drop a marble into the jar. Explain that when the jar is full (or when the marbles reach a certain level), the entire class will earn a reward.

- Be sure to add marbles throughout the day or students will lose interest. Mark lines on the jar with tape to note daily goals.

- Remember to restate the behavior you are reinforcing as you put the marble into the jar.

> "Billy has his book out already. That's a marble for the class."

Positive Behavior Bulletin Board

This is the most versatile classwide recognition system because you can tailor the theme to the interests of your students. Use your own creativity to create a colorful bulletin board that your students will enjoy.

Your bulletin board should include:

- The number of points needed to reach the class reward.

- A marker indicating number of points earned.

Each time you want to recognize good behavior, award a point by moving the marker forward. When the marker reaches the point goal, the class earns the reward. In the example below, the teacher has created a racetrack with 24 spaces. Each time the class demonstrates appropriate behavior, the teacher will move a marker one step closer to the finish line.

Positive recognition techniques are the most powerful behavior management tools you have as an educator. Your knowledge and skill in using these techniques will be one of the greatest determining factors towards your view of yourself as a professional and toward your students' achievement in school.

Skillful use of positive recognition means utilizing different approaches for individual students and situations. It means assessing each situation on its own merits and deciding how you, as the teacher, can best meet a student's needs.

The basis of these approaches is simply to treat students the way you would want a child of your own to be treated by a teacher.

Give some thought now to which positives you will want to incorporate into your classroom discipline plan. Be sure that praise is at the top of your list. And keep in mind that an extra benefit of being positive is that *your* day ends on a more positive note, too!

CHAPTER SIX — KEY POINTS

Positive Recognition

- Use positive recognition to encourage students to behave appropriately and to continue appropriate behavior.

- Increase a student's self-esteem through consistent, meaningful positive recognition. Let the student know you notice his or her efforts.

- Create a positive classroom environment for you and your students through consistent positive recognition.

- Consistent positive recognition will help you teach appropriate behavior and establish positive relationships with students.

- Praise students often. It's the most powerful, effective positive recognition you can give.

- Set a goal to send a specific number of positive notes home to parents each week.

- Set a goal to make a specific number of positive phone calls each week to parents.

- Recognize students' responsible behaviors with rewards.

- Motivate students through special privileges such as extra computer time or being class monitor.

- Use a classwide positive recognition system as a means to motivate all students to learn a new behavior or to work on a problem behavior that the group is having.

CHAPTER SEVEN

CREATING YOUR CLASSROOM DISCIPLINE PLAN

Part 3: Consequences

Children deserve structure.

Children deserve limits.

There is perhaps nothing more harmful we can do to children than allow them to disrupt or misbehave without showing them we care enough to let them know their behavior is not acceptable. Students need to learn that inappropriate behavior carries with it very real consequences. It's true in the real world, and they must learn this in the classroom.

As we have discussed before, it's your responsibility to let your students know what is acceptable and unacceptable behavior in your classroom.

We've looked at how your classroom rules will clearly tell students how they are expected to behave at all times in the classroom. And we've seen that consistent use of positive recognition will help motivate students to follow those rules.

There will be times, however, when students will choose not to follow the rules of the classroom—when they choose to keep you from teaching and other students from learning.

When this disruptive behavior occurs, you must be prepared to deal with it calmly and quickly.

Preparation is the key.

By carefully planning effective consequences, and by determining in advance what you will do when students misbehave, you will have a course of action to follow and will be able to avoid knee-jerk responses that are not in the best interests of you or your students.

Let's talk about what we mean by consequences.

We recommend that teachers follow these guidelines when choosing consequences for their classroom discipline plan.

- Consequences must be something that students do not like, but they must never be physically or psychologically harmful.

- Consequences are a choice.

- Consequences do not have to be severe to be effective.

Looking at each one of these guidelines, notice how each consequence is geared to help students choose appropriate behavior.

Consequences must be something that students do not like, but they must never be physically or psychologically harmful.

For a consequence to be effective, it must be an action that a student does not want—being last in line, getting time-out in the classroom, having to stay one minute after class, missing free time, having parents called, etc. But under no circumstances should a consequence in any way be physically or psychologically harmful to the student. Consequences should never be meant to embarrass or humiliate a student.

Above all, corporal punishment must never be used with students.

Over the years the Assertive Discipline program has been implemented in many ways by many different teachers. The vast majority have used the concepts appropriately and successfully. These teachers have been able to assume the confident leadership necessary to manage their classrooms, and in so doing motivate students to greater self-esteem and increased progress in school.

Unfortunately, there have been some exceptions. Of these exceptions, the one that concerns us the most is when educators have used the program in conjunction with corporal punishment or have used consequences to humiliate or degrade a child. Such actions are unconscionable to us. We feel that under no circumstances should an educator physically strike or humiliate a child.

Consequences are a choice.

If consequences are to be effective, if they are to be a helpful tool in teaching students how to behave in your classroom, they must be presented to students as a choice.

When we give students a choice, we place responsibility where it belongs, on the student.

Teacher: Carl, our classroom rule is to keep your hands to yourself. If you poke someone, you will choose to sit by yourself at the table. It's your choice.

Carl: Okay. (*Within a minute, Carl is poking the student next to him.*)

Teacher: Carl, you poked Fred. You have chosen to sit by yourself at the table.

By presenting your consequences as a choice, by allowing the student to choose that the consequence will occur, you no longer become the "bad guy" who gets the student in trouble. Instead, you've sent a powerful message to everyone.

The misbehaving student can no longer be seen as the victim of unfair teacher attention. *"She's so unfair. Carl didn't do anything. She's just out to get him."*

The teacher knows, the misbehaving student knows, and all the students in the classroom know: Carl was sitting by himself because of his misbehavior. It was his choice.

You must be consistent here, too. By assuring that an appropriate consequence always follows an infraction of a classroom rule, a teacher shows students that there is a relationship between how they choose to behave and the outcome of that behavior. This teaches students that they are accountable for their actions—that they can make important decisions over their own lives.

When you give students choices, they learn that they can be in control of what happens to them.

Remember, consequences are not punishment. Punishment is something that teachers *do* to students. Punishment takes the form of criticism, humiliation or even physical pain. Teachers who try to curb disruptive behavior with punishment do so at the expense of student self-esteem and growth. Punishment breeds resentment. It does not encourage students to take responsibility for choosing appropriate behavior.

Consequences, on the other hand, are actions students know will occur should they choose to break the rules of the classroom. Consequences must be seen as natural outcomes of inappropriate behavior.

Consequences do not have to be severe to be effective.

Many teachers believe the more harsh the consequence, the more effective it will be in curbing a student's misbehavior. Not true.

Keep this thought in mind when choosing your consequences: Your goal is to choose consequences that will work for everyone. For 70% of your students, a simple warning is all you'll ever have to give.

For another 20%, the consequences you choose do not have to be severe to be effective. The key to their effectiveness is that they are used consistently. It is the inevitability of the consequence, not the severity, that makes it effective. The most effective consequences are often the easiest to provide and the least time consuming to implement.

A fourth-grade teacher put it this way:

> "Most of the teachers at my school give very severe consequences when students misbehave. They have them stay in the classroom at recess, or stay after school and write sentences. The problem is that these consequences aren't always convenient for the teacher to implement. What happens then is that they aren't given consistently.

> "I found that all I need to do is have students work away from the rest of the class for five or ten minutes each time they misbehave. It's a lot easier on me than keeping students after class. It's a consequence I can administer immediately, and it works. But it works because I'm consistent about using it."

Here's another example that illustrates this concept, one that we find particularly interesting. This example shows how easy consequences can be to implement—how minimal they can be and yet still be effective.

These comments come from a veteran high school teacher:

> "After twenty years of working with kids, I've found the most effective consequence I can use is to keep a disruptive student one minute after class. One minute after class! That's all. It sounds like nothing, but it works like a charm. In high school, kids can't wait to leave class and be with their friends. That one minute delay really gets to them, believe me. Everybody's moved on and they're left behind. It wouldn't be any more effective if they had to wait twenty minutes.
>
> "The beauty of this consequence is that it's simple for me to use and it's effective."

Probably only 10% of your students will cause you real problems. Don't create your consequences with only these 10% in mind! Don't fall into the trap of making your consequences too severe.

Choosing Consequences for Your Classroom Discipline Plan: Establishing a Discipline Hierarchy

We've looked at what constitutes an appropriate consequence. Now let's look at how to use them. The best way is to organize the consequences you choose into a discipline hierarchy as part of your classroom discipline plan.

A discipline hierarchy lists consequences in the order in which they will be imposed for disruptive behavior within a day. The hierarchy is progressive, starting with a warning. The consequences then become gradually more substantial for the second, third, fourth, and fifth time that a student chooses to disrupt.

Here's what we mean:

- First Time a Student Disrupts

Most teachers **issue a warning** the first time a student disrupts or breaks a rule of the classroom.

> "Bob, the direction was to work without talking. That's a warning."

> "Colleen, the rule in this classroom is no running. That's a warning."

A warning gives the student an opportunity to choose more appropriate behavior before a more substantial consequence is received. It's a powerful reminder, one that carries an important message. The student knows that the next disruption will bring with it a real consequence.

- Second or Third Time a Student Disrupts

The second or third time a student disrupts in the same day, the teacher needs to **provide a consequence**. Make these consequences easy to implement, and not time consuming. Typical consequences for second or third infractions include time out, one-minute wait after class, and writing in a behavior log. (A detailed examination of each of these suggested consequences appears at the end of this chapter.)

- Fourth Time a Student Disrupts

You need to **contact parents** if a student disrupts a fourth time in a day.

Parent contact is a key component of managing student behavior. For some students, involving parents will be the only way you will motivate them to manage their own behavior. Teachers typically give the parent a call or send a note home, but there is an alternative method of parent contact that is very effective. One teacher described how she used it in her class.

"One of my students, Jason, had received his fourth consequence. In my class that means a call to parents. I told Jason that his parents had to be informed, and he was the one who was going to call them.

"At recess we went to the office. I picked up the phone, handed it to him and told him to call home and explain to his parents that his misbehavior had resulted in their being contacted. When he realized I was serious, his attitude changed.

"'Please give me another chance. I'll be good, I promise,' he said.

"I told him, 'Jason, this is the fourth time today I've had to deal with your misbehavior. You are going to call your parents and let them know about it. They need to know that your behavior is preventing me from teaching, you from learning, and is affecting other students' ability to learn as well.'

"Well, he made the call. It wasn't easy for him, and his parents weren't pleased. But this consequence definitely had an effect on him. Since that time, he's been choosing much more appropriate behavior. The very fact that he had to make the call placed responsibility right on his shoulders. It put him squarely in the middle of the situation. I don't think this fact was lost on him."

Regardless of whether the student calls the parent, you call the parent, or you send a note home, the point is that you let the parent know that a student's behavior is disruptive and cannot continue. Students need to know that you will be consistent in the enforcement of this consequence. And parents need to know where they fit in.

• Fifth Time a Student Disrupts

Sending a student **to the principal** should be the last consequence on your discipline hierarchy. In preparation for implementing this consequence, you must have already met with the principal and discussed actions he or she will take when students are sent to the office (see Chapter 17). You need to know that the administrator will provide the help and support you need. The principal's role might include counseling with the student, conferencing with the parents or suspending a severely disruptive student.

- ## Severe Clause

Sometimes you have to act quickly and decisively to stop a student's disruptive behavior. In cases of severe misbehavior, such as fighting, vandalism, defying a teacher or in some way stopping the entire class from functioning, a student would not receive a warning. He or she loses the right to proceed through the hierarchy of consequences. Severe misbehavior calls for an immediate consequence that will **remove the student from the classroom.**

On your discipline hierarchy this consequence is called a Severe Clause.

> A student becomes angry with a classmate and begins loudly yelling and punching him. The teacher walks up to the student and calmly states, "There is no fighting allowed in this classroom. You know the rule. You have chosen to go to the principal's office immediately. We will discuss this later."

Why is a Severe Clause necessary? If a student severely disrupts the classroom, he or she is stopping the education process. You are unable to teach and other students are unable to learn. Removing the student gives you back the control of the classroom and provides the disruptive student a chance to calm down before corrective measures are introduced. A Severe Clause addresses the severity of a student's actions. It sends a message that certain behaviors are totally beyond limits.

In Section Four we will look at more options for managing the behavior of difficult students.

Now let's look at some sample discipline hierarchies that adhere to the guidelines given.

Sample discipline hierarchy for grades K-3

First time a student breaks a rule:	Warning
Second time:	5 minutes working away from the group
Third time:	10 minutes working away from the group
Fourth time:	Call parents
Fifth time:	Send to principal
Severe Clause:	Send to principal

Sample discipline hierarchy for grades 4-6

First time a student breaks a rule:	Warning
Second time:	10 minutes working away from the group
Third time:	15 minutes working away from the group plus write in behavior journal
Fourth time:	Call parents
Fifth time:	Send to principal
Severe Clause:	Send to principal

Sample discipline hierarchy for grades 7-12

First time a student breaks a rule:	Warning
Second time:	Stay in class 1 minute after the bell
Third time:	Stay in class 2 minutes after the bell plus write in behavior journal
Fourth time:	Call parents
Fifth time:	Send to principal
Severe Clause:	Send to principal

You can see from these sample hierarchies that the consequences become more substantial each time a rule is broken. They follow a natural order that students will learn to expect.

The value of a discipline hierarchy as part of your classroom discipline plan is that everyone—students, parents, administrator, and, most importantly you—knows exactly what is going to happen each time a rule is broken.

You won't have to stop what you're doing and figure out what to do next.

Likewise, students will know exactly what they can expect each time they break a rule. The hierarchy becomes a tool for the student to learn self control.

This proactive planning increases your classroom management effectiveness. It assures that your responses will be consistent and fair no matter if you're tired, distracted, in a good mood or bad. It's a sure way to smoothly integrate behavior management into your teaching style.

Keeping Track of Consequences

For your discipline hierarchy to work, you will need a system to keep track of student misbehavior and consequences accrued. You'll need to know at a glance the names of students who have received consequences, and where the students are on the hierarchy.

More work for you? It doesn't have to be.

Some teachers use a clipboard to record students' names and the number of times they have broken a rule. Others record this information in their plan book or in a classroom management log book. Primary teachers often use a color-coded card system. Whatever system you use, it must be easily accessible to you as you teach. The easier it is, the less added work it will be for you.

Here is an example of how effective recordkeeping can work:

During class JoAnn is bothering another student. Her teacher calmly says to her, "JoAnn, the rule is 'Keep your hands and feet to yourself.' This is a warning." The teacher then writes JoAnn's name down on her clipboard.

Later in the same day, JoAnn begins talking loudly during quiet reading time. The teacher quietly reminds JoAnn, "This is the second time you have misbehaved. You have chosen to sit by yourself in the back of the room." The teacher then makes a check next to JoAnn's name to indicate that she has received the second consequence.

At the end of the day the teacher removes the sheet from the clipboard and places it in a permanent 3-ring binder, or transfers the information to her record book. The teacher then has permanent documentation of the student's misbehavior and how it was handled.

A Word about Names and Checks on the Board

Names and checks on the chalkboard are sometimes said to be essential to an Assertive Discipline program, but they are not. We originally suggested this particular practice after having watched teachers interrupt their lessons to make such negative comments to misbehaving students as, "You talked out again. I've had it. You're impossible. That's twenty minutes after school." We wanted to eliminate the need to stop the lesson and issue reprimands. Writing the student's name on the board would warn the student in a calm, nondegrading manner. It would also provide a recordkeeping system for the teacher. Unfortunately, some individuals have misinterpreted the use of names and checks on the board as a way of humiliating students. We now suggest that teachers write the disruptive student's name on a clipboard or in a record book and calmly say, for example, "Janet, you talked out. That's a warning."

Each student must start each day with a clean slate.

The consequences a student accumulates during one day should never roll over to the next day. You never want a student to think, "Well, I've already got two strikes against me from yesterday, so why should I behave today?" Keep sight of the fact that your goal is a positive one—for students to learn to manage their own behavior.

You and your students need to begin each day with the highest of expectations.

Suggested Consequences You May Want to Use in Your Own Classroom

Teachers have found these consequences to be effective in the discipline hierarchy, particularly the second or third time a student breaks a rule.

Time Out—Removing a Student from the Group

Removing a disruptive student from the group is not a new concept, but it is a very effective consequence for elementary age students. Designate a chair or table as the "time-out area." Depending upon the age of the student, a trip to the time-out area could last from five to ten minutes. (Note: It's very important that students not be isolated from the rest of the class for long lengths of time. Keep your time within these limits.)

While separated from the rest of the class, the student continues to do his or her classwork.

Use a time-out timer. It's hard to keep track of five or ten minutes when you're busy teaching class. Put a timer by the time-out area. When the student goes to the area, he or she turns the timer to the correct number of minutes. When the timer goes off, the student rejoins the class.

One-Minute Wait after Class

It sounds deceptively simple, but this is a consequence that students do not like and it works. You simply have the student wait one minute after the other students have been dismissed for recess, lunch, home, or the next period. One minute may not seem like a lot of time to you, but it can be an eternity to a student who wants to be first in line at handball, to lunch, on the bus, or who wants to walk to the next class with friends. Don't underestimate the power of this consequence. Secondary teachers in particular find it surprisingly effective.

During the one-minute wait you can take the opportunity to briefly counsel with the student regarding his or her disruptive behavior (see Chapter 12, Implementing Consequences). This consequence can be effective for all age levels.

Written Assignment in Behavior Journal

You want more from consequences than a student feeling contrite about what he did. You also want the student to learn from the experience. You want him to think about his behavior, and how he can choose to behave differently in the future.

When a student breaks a classroom rule, have him write an account of the misbehavior during recess, after class or at home. The account should include the following points:

1. Why the student chose to break the rule or not follow the direction.

2. What alternative action the student could have taken that would have been more appropriate.

The student should sign and date this page. The page should then be added to the student's documentation records. (It can also be sent home to parents as documentation of a student's misbehavior.)

This activity helps students accept responsibility for their behavior and think about choosing alternative behaviors in the future. This activity is appropriate for upper-elementary through middle-secondary students.

The behavior journal is the foundation of one ninth-grade science teacher's disciplinary consequences. Here's her rationale for using the journal:

> "I find there are so many students today who have not been taught to take responsibility for their behavior. It's our job as educators to teach them to take responsibility for their actions, to help them recognize the consequences their actions bring and to focus on teaching them alternative behaviors.

> "When a student is disruptive in my class, I ask him or her to write in the journal. I then use the journal as the focus for a meeting with the student to discuss how we can work together to improve his or her behavior.

> "These meetings are usually brief, to the point and highly effective. The student learns that I care, and that I expect him or her to take responsibility for his or her behavior.

> "If the meeting does not solve the problem, however, I'm prepared to take the next step. I ask the student to take the journal home to discuss with his or her parents. A parent is to sign the journal and return it to school.

> "Sending the journal home serves two purposes. First, the student does not enjoy showing it to parents or having to discuss his or her behavior. So it does serve as a deterrent. Second, the journal clearly documents to parents how their child is behaving. When and if I need to make a call to these parents, I know that they're already aware of a problem, and there will be much more support waiting."

There are other consequences that teachers find effective.
Among them:

- Detention

- Staying after school

- Loss of a special privilege

- Last to leave class

Whatever consequences you choose to give, choose ones that will work for you and your students.

- Consequences must be appropriate for your students, and you must feel comfortable using them.

- Choose consequences that are easy for you to implement.

- Choose consequences that your students will respond to.

- Don't choose consequences just because they've been suggested in a book, or because they work for other teachers. If you find consequences are difficult for you to use, you will be less inclined to administer them every time a student breaks a rule. So be realistic about your own abilities. Know what you really are willing to do.

Note: Misbehavior that occurs *outside* the classroom in common areas of the school must be addressed by a separate schoolwide discipline plan. A schoolwide discipline plan carries with it a separate set of consequences that students receive at the time of an infraction and does not impact your classroom discipline plan.

CHAPTER SEVEN — KEY POINTS

Consequences

- When disruptive behavior occurs, you must be prepared to deal with it calmly and quickly.

- You must be prepared by having in place consequences that students receive should they choose to disregard the rules of the classroom.

- Consequences:

  - are a choice.

  - do not work in isolation. They must be balanced with positive support.

  - do not have to be severe to be effective.

  - must be appropriate for your students, and you must be comfortable using them.

  - must be ones that students do not like, but they must never be physically or psychologically harmful.

  - should be organized into a hierarchy that clearly spells out what will happen from the first time a student breaks a rule to the fifth time the same student breaks a rule the same day.

- The first consequence should be a warning.

- Parent and administrator contact should appear near the end of the hierarchy.

- The hierarchy should include a Severe Clause for dealing immediately with severe misbehavior.

CHAPTER EIGHT

TEACHING YOUR CLASSROOM DISCIPLINE PLAN

Once you have decided upon your general classroom rules, the positive recognition you will use when rules are followed, and the consequences students will receive when they choose to break the rules, your classroom discipline plan is complete.

Now, in order to make the plan work effectively in your classroom, you must teach it to your students.

This is absolutely critical.

Don't just write your plan on a poster. Don't just read it to students. Teach your plan.

If you want students to learn an academic subject, you teach them. If you want students to behave, you have to teach them that, too. View the teaching of behavior in the same light as you view the teaching of academics. Teaching your discipline plan to your students is as important as any lesson you will teach during the year. This lesson should take place the first day of school (or, if you are introducing the discipline plan in the middle of the year, as soon as you have completed your plan).

Follow the guidelines presented in the sample lessons that follow. We've given you sample dialogue, but you should gear it to fit the needs and age of your own students. As you read, keep this thought in mind: All students, no matter their age, need a clear explanation of your rules, consequences and positive recognition at the start of the school year or at the introduction of the plan.

Our sample lessons are presented as follows:

Grades K-3   pages 98-104

Grades 4-6   pages 105-110

Grades 7-12   pages 110-114

Please turn to the lesson plan that applies to your own teaching situation.

Each lesson covers the following sequence:

1. Explain why you need rules.

2. Teach the rules.

3. Check for understanding.

4. Explain how you will reinforce students who follow the rules.

5. Explain why you have consequences.

6. Teach the consequences.

7. Check for understanding.

Teaching Your Classroom Discipline Plan to Students in Grades K-3

With younger students you will want to spend plenty of time teaching your lesson, making sure that all students understand the importance of each of your rules, and how they are to follow them. Examples, discussion and roleplay will enhance student participation and understanding. Likewise, young students must be just as clear about the role positive reinforcement and consequences play in your plan.

1. Explain why you need rules.

Teacher: How many of you have rules at home? (*Wait while students raise hands.*) Jennifer, thank you for raising your hand. What's a rule that you have at your home?

Jennifer: Play in the yard, not in the street.

Teacher: That's a really smart rule. Why do you think your mom wants you to follow this rule?

Jennifer: So I won't get hurt.

Teacher: That's right. She wants you to be safe, so she has rules that will help keep you safe. OK, who else wants to share a rule you have at home?

(*Continue sharing rules from home. Talk about why these rules are important to the safety and well being of the students. Tell students that just as it's important to have rules at home, it's also important to have rules at school.*)

Teacher: You have rules at home to keep you safe. We also have rules at school. Our school rules keep us safe, and also help us make sure that school is a good place for everyone to be, a place where we all can learn. Who can tell me some of the things that might happen at school if we didn't have any rules at all? (*Share responses.*)

2. Teach the rules.

Teacher: In our class we're going to have three very important classroom rules that I expect you to follow all the time.

One of the rules of our classroom will be "Walk , don't run, in the classroom." This is a very important rule for all of us. When you're at home do you ever run through the hall, or into the kitchen, or in your room? I'm sure you do! Now, look around you. I see lots of children, don't you? I see 28 children in this room! Now, do you have 28 children in your home? No, I don't think so. Twenty-eight is a lot of people. What could happen if all 28 of you were running around the classroom?

(Share responses.)

Teacher: That's right! Someone could trip. Someone might fall. Someone could get hurt. And it could get very noisy! Now, who can tell me why we have a rule "Walk, don't run, in the classroom?"

(Share responses.)

Roleplay the rule. Give students the opportunity to demonstrate following this rule.

Teacher: OK, let's practice following this rule. Sara, can you show us how to follow the rule, "Walk, don't run, in the classroom?" Good! Now I'm going to ask you to do something, and you will show us how to follow the rule. Ready? Sara, would you please put this book back in the reading corner?

(Sara picks up the book and walks back to the reading corner.)

Teacher: That's excellent! Thank you, Sara. Class, that's exactly how we all need to walk when we're in the classroom. Quietly and slowly. None of us were disturbed or bumped into, were we?

Continue teaching all of your rules in this manner.

3. Check for understanding.

Take the time to make sure all students understand the rules you've taught them.

Teacher:	Who can tell me again what our first classroom rule is? Stacy, can you tell me the rule? (*Stacy answers*.) That's very good! Thumbs up, class, if you agree with Stacy. That looks like everyone!
Teacher:	Jennifer, when is it OK to run in the classroom?
Jennifer:	Never!
Teacher:	Keith, if you need to get a sheet of paper in a big hurry, should you ever run to the paper box?
Keith:	No!
Teacher:	Good job! In a moment I'm going to ask everyone to line up at the door. When I say, "Line up," I want you to get up and walk to the door. I want to see everyone following our classroom rule, "Walk, don't run in the classroom."
	Ready? Class, line up at the door. (*Class lines up*.) Jeff is walking. So are Carla and Cecilia. Everyone is following the rule! Terrific! I know that all of you will be able to follow this classroom rule.

4. Explain how you will positively recognize students who follow the rules.

We have emphasized that positive recognition is the most important part of any behavior management plan. Now's the time to let your students know how much value you place on recognizing their good behavior.

Teacher: As my students, you are very important people in my life. I want to let you all know how much I care about you and how important it is to me that you have a year filled with learning and fun.

Now I want to tell you what will happen when you follow our classroom rules. The first thing you'll notice is that I'm going to really pay attention to good behavior. When I see you following the rules I won't ignore you. I'll let you know what a great job you're doing. I'll be sending notes home to your parents, telling them how terrific you've been. Sometimes I'll even give them a phone call! I'll be giving good behavior awards to you, too. I can promise you this: In my class, good behavior will get attention!

5. Explain why you have consequences.

Teacher: Some of you may be wondering what will happen if you do not follow our rules. That's a fair question. After all, none of us are perfect. We all have trouble at times following rules. Let's talk about this for a moment.

Who can tell me what might happen at home if you broke an important rule? Do your parents ever say, "No TV tonight" or "You can't play after school"? Why do your parents do this?

(*Share responses.*) Your parents do this to help you learn to behave in a safer way.

At school I want to help you learn to behave in a safe way also. When you break a classroom rule, you need to learn that something will happen. Something you probably won't like very much.

6. Teach the consequences.

Teacher: See this clipboard? (*Hold up clipboard.*) I'm going to keep it near me during the day. The first time you break a rule and disrupt the class, I will write your name down on the clipboard. I'll also remind you of what the rules are. For example, if you are running in the classroom, all I will say to you is, "John, the rule is no running in the classroom. That is a warning." If you are teasing your neighbor, I'll say, "Sarah, the rule is no teasing. That's a warning."

That's all that I'll do.

This warning gives you a chance to choose better behavior. And I know that you will choose better behavior.

But, if you do break this rule again, or any other rule during the day, I'll put a check next to your name. (*Show check next to name on clipboard.*) This means that you've broken a rule two times. And this means that you have chosen to sit for five minutes in the time-out area. This will give you time to calm down and think about your behavior.

The second time you break a rule in this class you will go to the time-out area.

Go through the rest of the discipline hierarchy in this manner, explaining each consequence. Afterwards, take the time to emphasize your belief that the students can behave and can act responsibly.

Teacher:	I know that all of you can follow our classroom rules. I know that all of you can make good decisions about when it's appropriate to talk, when you do your work, and when you are with your friends. I hope that none of you choose to go to time out, have me call your parents, or go to the principal.

7. Check for Understanding

Teacher:	Do any of you have a question about what will happen when you break a rule in the classroom?
	Who can tell me the first thing I will do when a rule is broken?
	(*Ask students to respond.*)
Keith:	We get a warning.
Teacher:	That's right, Keith. I'll give a warning. The helpful thing about a warning is that it gives you a chance to stop, think about your behavior, and make a better choice. Now, what happens the second time a rule is broken?

Make sure that all students understand what will happen each time a rule is broken during the day. With young students, you will have to review the consequences frequently.

Teaching Your Classroom Discipline Plan to Students in Grades 4-6

Students in grades 4-6 want to understand the reasons behind your classroom rules. Explain why they need rules, and how your rules will help them do better in school. Relate how rules will affect them in other areas of their lives.

1. Explain why you need rules.

Teacher: I want to make sure this is a great year for all of you. I also want to make sure all of you are able to learn as much as you possibly can. To make certain this happens, we need to talk about how I expect you to behave in my classroom.

                    This is important because in my class you have the right to learn in a safe and pleasant classroom. To make sure that all students can enjoy this right, you have the responsibility to follow our classroom rules.

Talk about other rules students have in their lives. Ask students to share some of the rules they have at home.

Teacher: What are some of the rules that you have at home? Why do you think that you have these rules at home? Are these rules important? Why?

                    Now what are some other rules you've had to follow? (*Talk about rules that students have experienced outside the home as well: traffic rules, safety rules at theaters, camp, after-school programs, etc.*) Why have these rules? Why are these rules enforced?

Tell students that just as it's important to have rules at home, or to have traffic rules, it's also important to have rules at school.

Teacher: Why do you think we have to have rules at school? (*Share comments.*) Having rules will help everyone have a safer, better time in school. Also, when we have rules, you will know exactly how I expect you to behave. You'll never have to say, "I didn't know we weren't supposed to . . ."

2. Teach the rules.

Teacher: The first rule we have in our classroom is "Follow directions." During the day, I'll be asking you to do lots of different things. I'll be giving you many, many directions. Can anyone give me some ideas of what those things might be?

(*Share responses: For example, pass your papers forward, clear your desks, go to your reading groups, take your books out.*)

That's right! I'll be giving lots of directions just like these every day. Why do you think it's important that you follow my directions when I give them?

(*Share responses.*)

It is important that you follow these directions for a lot of reasons. For one thing, following directions helps us to be safe. If I dismiss you for recess and everyone races for the door, someone might get hurt. Following directions also helps us all do what we're supposed to do—quickly and without a lot of wasted time. We've got so much to do each day, and I want to be sure we get it all done! When I give a direction, I need you to follow it immediately.

3. Check for understanding.

Teacher: Now let's take a minute to review what a direction is. How can you be sure when I am giving you a direction? Kenny, what's a direction?

Kenny: When you tell us to do something.

Teacher: That's right. A direction is any time I ask you to do something. Now, class, please clear your desks. Put everything away.

(Pause. Look around the room.)

Jessica's putting her things away. Good job following directions! Candy and Shannon are clearing their desks. So is Joe. It looks like everyone has followed this direction! You listened. You followed the direction. And now we're all ready to do whatever's coming up next! See how well we can get things done? I know all of you can follow this rule.

Continue in this manner teaching each of your classroom rules. To help students remember the rules, place a chart on the wall or write the rules on the board.

4. Explain the positive recognition you will use when students follow the rules.

Positive recognition is the most important part of any behavior management plan. Now's the time to let your students know how much value you place on recognizing their good behavior. The positive recognition you give will encourage them to repeat the behavior.

Teacher: Now I want to tell you what will happen when you choose to follow our classroom rules. You'll notice right away that I'm going to pay a lot of attention to good behavior. When I see you following the rules I won't ignore you. I'll let you know what a great job you're doing. I'll be sending notes home to your parents, telling them how terrific you've been. Sometimes I'll even give them a phone call! I'll be giving awards to you, too, for good behavior. The point is this: I care about each and every one of you. And I know that you can and will follow our rules. When you do, it will be my pleasure to recognize your good work.

5. Explain why you have consequences.

Teacher: You're probably wondering what will happen when you break one of our classroom rules. This is what will happen: When you choose to break a rule, and it *is* your choice, you will receive a consequence.

(*Pause.*)

Teacher: Why do you think I have to offer you consequences for your actions? Because I have to be able to help you make better choices. You all are becoming responsible young people. I want to help you make good choices—and sometimes you need to understand that when you don't make good choices, things will happen that you won't like.

In this class I have what I call a discipline hierarchy. This hierarchy lets all of us know what will happen if you disrupt one time during the day and what will happen the second time, third time, fourth time and fifth time you disrupt.

> This is my discipline hierarchy. (*Put up poster listing all consequences, or write them on the board. The hierarchy should be left up for students to become familiar with.*)

6. Teach the consequences.

Teacher: Let's read through the hierarchy together. James, would you please read it for us?

(James reads.)

Teacher: Thank you, James. OK, class, those are the consequences. Now let's talk about how we'll use them.

See this clipboard? (*Hold up.*) The first time you have trouble, I will write your name down on the clipboard. I'll also remind you of what the rules are. For example, if you are talking when you should be doing independent seatwork, all I will say to you is, "John, the rule is no talking during seatwork. That is a warning." That's all that I'll do.

If you have trouble following this or another rule during the day, I'll put a check next to your name. This means that you have chosen to receive a consequence. As you can see on the discipline plan, that consequence is to sit for five minutes away from the group. This will give you time to calm down and think about your behavior.

Go through the rest of this disciplinary hierarchy in this manner, explaining each consequence. Afterwards, emphasize your belief that the students can behave and can act responsibly.

Teacher: I believe that all of you can follow our classroom rules. I have confidence that all of

you can make good decisions to choose
behavior that makes our classroom a place
where we all can learn and get along together. I
hope that none of you will choose to remain
after class, have me call your parents, or go to
the principal.

7. Check for understanding.

Question students to make sure they understand the consequences,
and how the hierarchy works. Make sure that students understand
that these consequences will be given every time they choose to
misbehave. Students must learn that the consequences are inevitable.
With this knowledge they will learn that they are accountable for
their actions and have control over the consequences by the way
they choose to behave.

Teacher: Now, are there any questions about how I am
going to use the disciplinary hierarchy in my
classroom? (*Answer any questions.*) Remember,
these consequences will be given every time
you choose to misbehave.

Teaching Your Classroom Discipline Plan to Students in Grades 7-12

For students in grades 7-12, teach your rules in a more matter-of-fact
manner. These students have been exposed to classroom rules
before, so you can be brief and to the point. Give a brief rationale
for each rule and state your expectation that all students will follow
the rules. To make your lesson as meaningful as possible, relate
rules to the real world that they'll soon be entering.

Keep in mind that secondary teachers often make the erroneous
assumption that students should just know how to behave.
Remember, your classroom is unique and you have your own
unique set of expectations that need to be communicated.

1. Explain why you need rules.

Teacher: In this classroom I have three rules that will be in effect at all times. I'll explain the rules in just a moment. First, though, I want all of you to clearly understand why I have rules.

It's simple. I need to be able to teach, and you need to be able to learn. For both of those actions to happen, we all need appropriate behavior in the classroom. I know you're familiar with following rules. You have to follow traffic rules if you want to drive. You have to follow your boss's rules when you're at work. These rules are in place for safety reasons, and to help get a job done. It's no different in class. I have rules so we can get our job done here. And just as you have to follow traffic rules, and rules on the job, I expect you to follow the rules in my classroom.

2. Teach the rules.

Teacher: My first rule is, "Follow directions." This means that when I give any direction to you, such as to open your books, take out your notebooks, or pass your papers forward, I expect you to follow the direction immediately.

We have lots to do in this class, and I don't want to waste any of your time or mine asking over and over again for something to be done. When I give a direction, I expect you to follow it.

Continue explaining each of the rules.

3. Check for understanding.

Teacher: Does anyone have any questions about these rules?

4. Explain the positive recognition you will use.

Teacher: Now that we've talked about the classroom rules, let's talk about what happens when you follow these rules. I'm a lot more interested in recognizing you for appropriate behavior than I am in pointing out inappropriate behavior. You'll notice this year that I'll be on the lookout for students who follow the rules, and I will let you know that I appreciate your efforts.

Throughout the year, I'll be passing out coupons for the student store, sending notes home to parents, and letting you know in other ways that I recognize the fact that you're choosing to follow the rules of this classroom. I just think it makes sense to let you know that you're doing a good job. We all like a pat on the back once in awhile, and I plan to be giving a lot of those this year!

5. Explain why you have consequences.

Teacher: I expect all of you to follow the rules of the classroom. But to be realistic, it may not always work out that way. You are young adults now, and you are responsible for your behavior. When you make poor choices in what you do, oftentimes there are consequences. It's true in the workplace, it's true at home, and it's true here at school.

6. Teach the consequences.

Teacher: In this classroom I have what I call a discipline hierarchy. You can see it posted on the wall in front of the room. (*Point to hierarchy.*) As you can see, the hierarchy clearly spells out what will happen the first time a rule is broken, the second time, third time, fourth and fifth time.

Let's go through it. Follow along, please.

The first time you choose to disrupt, I will write your name down and you will be given a warning. That's it. This warning is your chance to stop, think and change your behavior.

The second time you break the same rule, or any other rule in the same day, you will stay after class one minute past the bell.

The third time you disrupt, you'll stay in class two minutes after the bell.

The fourth time, I call your parents. No if's, and's, or but's. This is a hard and fast rule. Four disruptions in one day is completely unacceptable and your parents will be called.

The fifth time, you will be sent to the principal.

You'll also see that I have listed a Severe Clause. This means that in cases of severe misbehavior, such as fighting or talking back, you will not have the privilege of working your way through the hierarchy. You will go straight to the principal.

I have confidence that every one of you can make good decisions about how you behave in school. You know what's expected of you. I want to see you live up to these expectations.

7. Check for understanding.

Question students to make sure they understand the consequences and how the hierarchy works. Make sure that students understand that these consequences will be given every time they choose to misbehave. Students must learn that the consequences are inevitable.

With this knowledge they will learn that they are accountable for their actions and have control over the consequences by the way they choose to behave.

> Teacher: Are there any questions? If not, I will assume then that all of you understand how I will be dealing with misbehavior in this classroom.

Note: When you teach your plan, be sure to relate rules, positive reinforcement and consequences to elements that matter in the students' own lives. Grades K-3 will respond to home analogies. Grades 4-9 will benefit from a discussion that includes peer relationships. High school students can understand expectations in terms of the workplace.

Continue to Communicate Your Plan

Post your discipline plan in the classroom where it will serve as a continuing, helpful reminder of your rules, positive recognition and consequences.

Send a copy of your classroom discipline plan, along with a letter of explanation, home to parents. Ask parents to review the plan with their children and send a signed portion of the letter back to school. (See Chapter 17 for a sample discipline plan letter to parents.)

CHAPTER EIGHT — KEY POINTS

Teaching Your Classroom Discipline Plan

- Create lessons to teach your students your classroom discipline plan.

- Explain to students why you need rules.

- Teach the rules.

- Explain how you will positively recognize students who follow the rules.

- Explain why you have consequences.

- Teach the consequences.

- As soon as you've taught the lesson, immediately begin reinforcing students who follow the rules.

- Review rules frequently at the start of the year. Review as needed as the year progresses.

- Post your discipline plan in the classroom.

- Send a copy of your classroom discipline plan home to parents.

TEACHING RESPONSIBLE BEHAVIOR

TEACHING RESPONSIBLE BEHAVIOR

Developing your classroom discipline plan, and teaching your plan to your students, are the first steps in empowering them to choose the responsible behavior that will enable them to succeed in school. The next step is to teach them how to make responsible behavioral choices in all situations at school.

In this section we will share a variety of techniques that will help you motivate the majority of your students to behave appropriately.

Finally, we will examine three scenarios in which successful teachers put all of these guidelines and techniques together to create a smoothly running classroom in which behavior management efforts are an integral part of the overall teaching process.

TEACHING RESPONSIBLE BEHAVIOR

Part 1: Determining and Teaching Specific Directions

The beginning of the school year is filled with "first times" for students.

First time to line up for recess.

First time to go to reading or math groups.

First time to return to class after lunch.

First time to collect and pass out papers.

First time to work in a lab situation.

First time to work in a cooperative learning group.

What happens the first time your students have to do any of these activities? Do they know how you expect them to proceed? Do *you* know how you expect them to proceed?

> "The first day of school, when the ten o'clock bell rang, I announced, 'recess time.' Instead of lining up at the door like I assumed they would, thirty-five kids stampeded out to the playground. Fortunately no one was hurt in the rush, but I learned a good lesson about assumptions. I assumed they'd line up. They assumed that they could race out the door. We were all mistaken!"

It's important that all of your directions are clear if you are going to make the most effective use of your classroom discipline plan.

Here's why:

> Your classroom discipline plan spells out the general rules of your classroom—rules that are in effect at all times. The most important of these rules is, "Follow directions." This rule is included to ensure that students promptly follow *any* direction you might give during the day.
>
> To comply with this rule and meet your expectations, students must understand what each and every specific direction you give means.
>
> You can't assume when you enter into a new activity or procedure anytime during the year that your students will know how to behave the way you want them to.
>
> You would never make this assumption about math competency or reading skills. Why assume that your behavioral expectations are obvious? After all, every teacher has different ways of moving into groups, collecting work, distributing assignments, etc. Your students need to follow *your* expectations, not another teacher's expectations.

Highly successful teachers—right at the beginning of the year—take time to teach their students exactly how they want them to behave in all classroom situations. They teach and reteach their expectations until every student in the class knows exactly how to handle every single activity or procedure—until all students know *how* to line up for recess, *how* to go to learning groups, and *how* to return to class after lunch.

Teaching specific directions will take time and effort, but the results are worth it.

In the past, have you found yourself constantly repeating directions over and over and over until it nearly drives you crazy?

The more time you put in at the beginning of the year teaching directions, the less time you'll have to spend repeating them as the year goes by.

You can prevent problems throughout the year by teaching your specific directions at the beginning of the year.

To plan your specific directions, you need to do two things:

> First, **identify** the academic activities, routine procedures and special procedures for which specific directions are needed.

> Next, **determine** the specific directions you want your students to follow for each activity and procedure you've identified.

Let's look more closely. . .

Identify the academic activities, routine procedures and special procedures for which you need to determine specific directions.

Here are examples of academic activities:

- When you are giving a directed lesson in front of the class

- When students are doing independent seat work

- When students are working in small groups doing cooperative learning tasks

- When the class is having a group discussion

- When students are taking a test

- When students are working at centers or in lab activities

Here are examples of some routine procedures:

- When students enter the classroom

- When students leave the classroom

- When a student wants a drink of water

- When a student needs to use the restroom

- When a student needs to sharpen his pencil

- When students turn in homework

- When the teacher gives a signal to begin an activity

- When students transition from one activity to another

Special procedures:

- When the fire drill bell rings

- When the class goes to a school assembly

- When the class goes on a field trip

- When guests come to the classroom

- When students are at the library

Note: Music teachers, art teachers, PE teachers and teachers who work in other special situations have to come up with a list of the activities and procedures that apply to their students.

For example:

- Putting music equipment away

- Putting sports equipment away

- Cleaning up after an art activity

Think about a typical week in your own classroom. Start at the beginning of the school day on Monday and work your way through to the end of the day on Friday. Identify the academic activities, routine procedures and special procedures (if any) your students will be engaged in. Try not to leave anything out.

Remember, when you give any direction in class, you're expecting 10, 20 or 30 students to follow it. So, don't assume that behavioral expectations for any activity or procedure are obvious. It's not likely that 30 or more students will instinctively go about following any direction in exactly the same way.

The time you take to plan your specific directions for all activities and procedures will be more than made up when students are able to follow those directions quickly and without confusion or question.

Keep in mind that your ultimate goal is not to control behavior, but to help your students succeed at their various activities.

Determine the specific directions you want your students to follow for each procedure and activity.

> "Most of my students this year came from a classroom where the teacher really didn't mind a lot of noise and moving around. That's fine for him, but I can't teach that way. I need to know that my classroom will be quiet when I need it to be."
>
> *–Fifth-grade teacher*

When determining the specific directions you want your students to follow, use these guidelines:

- Choose only a limited number of specific directions for each classroom activity.

- Your directions must be observable and easy for students to follow. Don't include vague directions such as "act good" or "behave appropriately."

- Relate your directions to:

  - how you want students to participate in the activity or procedure—*what you expect them to do.*

  - how you expect students to *behave* in order to be successful in the activity.

Remember, you're setting up your classroom environment for the year. It's up to you to decide how you want your students to behave during each academic activity and routine procedure. Visualize each activity and think about each of the directions you'd like your students to follow when engaged in that activity.

Here are some examples of specific directions that adhere to the guidelines given:

Academic Activity: When the teacher is giving a directed lesson in front of the class.

1. Clear your desks of everything but paper and pencil.

2. Eyes on me, or eyes on your paper. No talking while I'm talking.

   (These directions let students know what they are expected to do.)

3. Raise your hand and wait to be called upon to ask or answer a question. Don't shout out answers.

   (This direction lets students know how you expect them to behave.)

Academic Activity: When students are working independently at their desks.

1. Have all necessary books, paper, pencils and other materials on your desk.

2. Begin working on your assignment as soon as you receive it.

    (These directions let students know what they are expected to do.)

3. No talking. Raise your hand to ask a question.

    (This direction lets students know how you expect them to behave.)

Routine Procedure: When students enter the classroom.

1. Walk into the room.

2. Go directly to your seat and sit down.

    (These directions let students know what they are expected to do.)

3. No talking after the bell rings.

    This direction lets students know how you expect them to behave.

Special Procedure: Assemblies

1. Put books and materials away.

2. Without talking, walk at a normal pace to the door. Line up in single file. No talking in line.

3. Line leader opens the door. Without talking, class walks to the cafeteria.

4. No talking during the assembly.

5. Return to class in a single line. No talking.

Remember, this is your opportunity to create a classroom environment that reflects your teaching style and is conducive to learning, so be sure your specific directions reflect this. Be creative, be unique, be specific according to your own wants and needs.

The Difference Between Rules and Directions

- Rules are posted in your classroom, and are in effect at all times during the day.

- Directions are in effect for the duration of a specific activity.

- Directions may change based on the needs of the teacher and maturity level of the students.

Teach Your Specific Directions

Teaching specific directions is as important as teaching any academic lesson. Teaching your specific directions ensures that behavior problems will be reduced during all academic activities, routine procedures and special procedures. Teaching specific directions also increases a student's opportunity to succeed at those activities.

Once you've established your specific directions, your goal in teaching them is not to simply pass along instructions, but to make this process a learning experience for students as well. Involve students. Teach them why your directions are important to everyone's well being.

When students understand the reasons behind your directions, they'll be much more likely to follow them.

Preparing to teach specific directions

As in any other kind of lesson, preparation is the key to successful implementation.

You need to prepare a lesson for each direction you will teach. Plan the lesson with the same care that you would plan a lesson for any academic subject. What is your objective? What behavior do you want the students to learn? What specific directions do you want your students to follow? How will you reinforce each lesson?

Plan to teach each specific direction immediately prior to the first time the activity or procedure takes place.

This means, of course, that during the first days of school you will be teaching many specific directions for various activities and procedures. Though this may seem like a lot of work, don't let that deter you. The benefits of your efforts will be reduced behavior problems throughout the year.

Here are two ideas you may want to incorporate into lessons on specific directions:

1. Just as you use visual aids in presenting academic material, it's often a good idea to do the same when you teach directions. A visual reminder will help students focus on your words and remember what you've said. Posters or flipcharts are helpful for older students. Younger non-readers will benefit from simple drawings on posters. Don't underestimate the value of these reminders to secondary students, either. Everyone needs a reminder now and then. Creating these visuals will take some time, but it's time you'll easily make up as the year proceeds with fewer disruptions. Laminate your charts and plan to use them year after year, updating as necessary.

   After you present your lesson, post some of these reminders in the classroom. (Post those directions that students need the most help in remembering, or that you feel are most important. Keep them up to date and change as needed.) Giving students visual clues for appropriate behavior will help reinforce your directions. This is a helpful suggestion for students of all ages.

2. It's a good idea to teach students a name for each activity or procedure. The goal of teaching specific directions is for students to make transitions quickly and without confusion or disorder. Therefore, it is important that you are able to communicate each direction as clearly as possible.

It will be a lot easier for students to move quickly when they hear, for example, "Journal time" than if they hear, "OK students, let's spend some time now writing in our journals."

Decide on names for activities and be consistent in their use. These names will serve as cues that students can follow quickly and easily.

Examples:

Seat work	Reading groups
Journal time	SSR (Sustained silent reading)
Independent work	Directed lesson
Assembly	Lab groups
Flag salute	Computer room

Now let's look at how teachers at different grade levels successfully teach their specific directions.

Use the following lessons as a guideline for developing a lesson for any specific direction. Keep in mind that your own lessons will differ, based on the age of your students and the directions you are teaching, but the focus of explanation, teaching and checking for understanding remain the same.

Age-Appropriate Guidelines for Teaching Specific Directions

Grades K-3

With younger students you will want to spend plenty of time teaching and reinforcing each specific direction lesson. Give students the opportunity to roleplay the directions, and give them ample opportunities to follow the directions after the lesson is given. Reteach and reinforce often. Use pictures or other visual clues to help reinforce the directions.

Grades 4-6

Students in grades 4-6 want to understand the reasons behind the directions they are expected to follow. Explain why they need to follow this direction and what the benefit will be to them and the other students.

Grades 7-12

Teach your specific directions in a matter-of-fact manner to students in this age group. Let them clearly know why you expect these directions to be followed.

Teaching Specific Directions in Grades K-3

Specific Directions for Responding When the Teacher Signals for Attention

1. Explain rationale for the direction.

> Teacher: There will be times during the day when I'm going to need all of you to stop what you're doing and give me your complete attention—times when I'll need to know that everyone is listening to me.
>
> When I need everyone's attention, I'm going to give you a **signal** (*for example, ringing a bell, turning a flashlight on and off*).

2. Involve the students by asking questions.

Teacher: Who can tell me what a signal is? What are some other signals that you know about?

(*Share responses: police siren, fire siren, crossing lights, car horn, yard bell*)

Teacher: Why do you think we have signals? (Signals are a way of getting our attention.)

(*Ask students when they think a signal might be needed in class.*)

Teacher: I need to have a signal in the classroom, too. When I need your attention, I have to have a way to let you know.

When are some of the times that I'll need to use this signal in class? When is it important that I get your attention?

(*Share responses: when we need to stop one activity and start another; when it's time to clean up; when you have an important idea you want to tell us, etc.*)

Teacher: Those are all excellent reasons. And I think that you can see why I'll need to use a signal. A signal lets everyone know that it's time to stop what we're doing and pay attention to me.

3. Explain the specific directions.

The teacher then explains his own signal.

Teacher: When I want your attention, I will ring this small bell.

When I give this signal, I want you to do three things.

1. Stop whatever you're doing.

2. Look at me.

3. Listen to me.

Stop, look and listen. Don't turn around to your neighbor. Don't move around the room. Wait for me to give directions.

4. Check for understanding.

The teacher checks for understanding by asking several students to restate the direction. He then reinforces the directions by writing them on the board. With K-1 students, the teacher instead might show a poster showing a stop sign (stop), an eye (look), and an ear (listen).

Teacher: Now, who can raise his or her hand and tell me what you are to do first when I ring the bell?

(As students state the directions, the teacher writes them on the board.)

Next, have the students practice or roleplay the directions.

Teacher: Let's see how well we've learned this signal. Right now we're going to practice what you'll do when I give the signal. I want all of you to take out your science books. Turn to the top of page 11 and begin reading. (*Students comply.*)

When I give the signal, I expect you to stop, look and listen. All right. Everyone begin working.

> *(Students begin working. In a few minutes, the teacher gives the signal by ringing the bell. The teacher immediately begins to praise those students who are following the direction.)*

Teacher: Marcia has stopped what she's doing. Bob has his eyes on me. Pat is listening. Good work!

Now, does anyone have any questions about how to follow my signal?

Teaching Specific Directions in Grades 4-6

Specific Directions for a Seat Work Activity

1. Explain rationale for the directions.

Teacher: During the year, I am often going to ask you to do work at your desk. I call this **seat work**. Doing seat work means working on your own at your desk. You may be reading. You may be writing. You may be working on a math problem. Whatever it is that you're doing, you're doing it *on your own.*

To make sure you understand exactly how I expect you to behave during seat work I am going to teach you the directions I expect you to follow. It's important that everyone follows these directions because everyone needs to be able to do their work in a quiet environment.

2. Explain the directions.

Teacher: I've listed the directions for seat work here. *(Points to chart.)* Let's look at the first one. When I tell you it's time for seat work, I expect you first to put all necessary books, paper, pencils and other materials you'll need on your desk. I also expect you to clear your desk of any other materials you won't be using.

Now let's look at the second direction. (*Points to direction #2 on chart.*) "Stay in your seat and begin working on your own as soon as you receive the assignment." That means no wandering around. No working on other classwork. No reading a library book.

The third direction for seat work is (*points to chart*), "If you need help, or want to ask a question, raise your hand." I will come over to you, or ask you to come to my desk.

Finally, the fourth direction (*points to chart*) is, "No talking during seat work." Seat work is quiet time.

3. Check for understanding.

Teacher: Now, I want to make sure that I was very clear in explaining these directions for seat work, and that everyone understands what I expect of you. Can someone raise his or her hand and tell me, in your own words, what I mean by the first direction, "Have all necessary materials on your desk?"

Student: You mean that we have to take out all of the stuff we'll need for doing the assignment, like paper, and pencils, and books, and put them on our desks.

Teacher: You did a good job of listening. Can someone explain the next direction (*points to chart*), "Stay in your seat and begin working on your assignment on your own as soon as you receive it"?

Student: That means we need to begin working as soon as we get the assignment. You can't get up and talk to your friends.

Teacher: Exactly right! Can someone now explain what I mean by this direction (*points to third direction*), "If you have a question, or need help, raise your hand and wait until the teacher calls on you"?

Student: That means that if you don't understand the assignment, or if you need help on a problem or something, you should raise your hand and wait for the teacher to call your name. Then the teacher will either come to your desk or you will go up to hers.

Teacher: Do any of you have questions about what I want you to do when you are doing seat work?

Student: What if I need to sharpen my pencil?

Teacher: We have already learned this direction, but let's review it. If you need to get a sharpened pencil, raise your dull pencil in the air. When I give you permission, you may place your pencil in the "dull" pencil cup and take a sharpened pencil from the cup marked "sharpened." Then return immediately to your seat and begin working.

Teaching Specific Directions in Grades 7-12

Specific Directions for a Directed Lesson

1. Present rationale for directions.

Teacher: When I'm speaking in front of the class, giving a lecture, I need you to behave in a way that I can teach and everyone can learn. For that reason, I'm going to tell you exactly how I expect you to behave during a lecture.

2. Explain the specific directions.

Teacher: These are the directions I expect you to follow when I'm speaking.

1. Clear your desks of everything but paper and pencil.

I don't want anything out except paper for taking notes and a pencil to write with.

2. Eyes on me, or eyes on your paper.

During a lecture you need to either be looking at me or looking at your paper as you write. Eyes on me. Eyes on your paper.

3. Raise your hand and wait to be called upon to ask or answer a question.

If you want to ask me a question, answer a question, or respond to something another student has said, you need to raise your hand.

3. Check for understanding.

Teacher: I think these directions are clear enough. Who can tell me what I expect you to do during a lecture?

(The teacher asks for volunteers to restate directions).

Immediately follow up any specific direction lesson with the activity or procedure that has just been taught. Be sure to reinforce students who follow the directions appropriately, and provide reminders (or reteach if necessary) to those students who don't.

Review the specific directions for each activity as long as is necessary.

Depending on the age and ability of your students, you may find it necessary to occasionally review specific directions, especially at the beginning of the school year or just before an activity that the students haven't done in a long time.

At the beginning of the school year, review the directions each time you begin a different routine procedure or academic activity. As the year proceeds, you'll know when you need to review. If students aren't following directions, review them.

It can be as simple as going over the directions charts or asking students to state the rules aloud for the rest of the class.

Guidelines for Reviewing Specific Directions

First Two Weeks   Review directions each time the class engages in the activity.

First Month   Review directions each Monday (as a reminder and refresher for the week to come).

Remainder of Year   Review directions as needed. It is especially important to review directions after a vacation, on special days when students are especially keyed up (the first snowfall, Halloween, field-trip day) or whenever the class engages in a new activity.

CHAPTER NINE — KEY POINTS

Specific Directions

- Don't assume that students know how you want them to behave in all of the situations that occur during a normal school day. These expectations must be taught.

- Identify the classroom situations for which specific directions are needed. Then determine those directions.

- Teach your specific directions immediately prior to the first time the activity takes place.

- Teach the lesson with the same care you would any academic lesson.

- Explain your rationale for teaching the direction.

- Explain the directions.

- Check for understanding.

- Review the specific directions for each activity as long as is necessary.

- Post visual clues (charts, posters, illustrations) around the classroom to help remind students of appropriate behavior during different activities and procedures.

TEACHING RESPONSIBLE BEHAVIOR

Part 2: Using Positive Recognition to Motivate Students to Behave

Now that you've determined directions for each classroom situation—and have taught those directions to your class—your goal is to help students achieve success in following those directions. Positive recognition of a student's appropriate behavior is the most effective way to achieve this goal. In this chapter we will present some positive recognition techniques that will help you teach your students to choose to behave responsibly.

We will focus on four areas:

- Using positive repetition to motivate students to follow directions and get on task.

- Using positive recognition to keep students on task.

- Implementing classwide positive recognition systems.

- Increasing your consistency in using positive reinforcement.

How to Use Praise to Motivate Students to Follow Directions and Get On Task

Positive Repetition

During the course of the day you'll be giving your students many different directions. You've taught your students your specific directions, but experience has shown you that some of your students still may not follow them.

What happens next? Here's what often happens:

The teacher immediately focuses on students who *aren't* doing what they should be doing.

> "Seth, get back to your seat and start working on your assignment. Stop acting silly."

> "Carol, stop talking to your neighbor. Get back to work."

> "Jaime, put your math book away and get out your social studies book. You're wasting time!"

The teacher focuses on the negative. The teacher points out those students who are misbehaving.

What message does this give your students? It says the teacher is *looking for* misbehavior. *Expecting* misbehavior. Ready and waiting to pounce on students who don't follow the directions.

By focusing on students who are not following directions, a teacher can create a negative environment in the classroom.

> *"Don't do this!" "Stop that!"* And the students get the message that the best way to attract attention is by engaging in inappropriate behavior. Students who do meet expectations are generally ignored.

As an educator, and leader, be careful about the examples you are setting for your students.

Giving them the impression that students who disobey are going to be the ones who get the attention is not the message you want to communicate.

A more successful approach would be to keep the emphasis on the positive by looking for success. Praise students who are doing what is expected.

For example:

A teacher gives a direction:

> "Class, please line up for recess."

Now she immediately looks for students who are behaving appropriately and points out their actions.

> "Jimmy is lining up quietly. Ellen is in line, too."

Negative focus or positive? Which kind of response fills the room with motivation? Which fills the room with positive energy? Which response is less stressful for the teacher to make and students to receive? Most important, which response focuses the *other* students on the appropriate behavior?

What do you want for your classroom, for your students? You have a choice. You can focus on negative behavior. Or you can redirect that behavior through positive support.

Be positive. Praise students. Look for what's working in your classroom, and acknowledge it! It's simply a matter of viewing your classroom activities in a positive manner and following these guidelines for using the **positive repetition** technique. Here's how positive repetition works:

Positive Repetition

1. Give a direction.

2. Immediately look for at least two students who are following the direction.

3. Say the students' names and restate the direction as they are following it.

This technique positively reinforces students who are following the directions, and gives a positively stated reminder to those students who are not yet following the directions.

Here are examples of positive repetition in action:

Direction:	"Take your places on the reading mat."
Positive repetition:	"Jennifer and Danny are already at their places on the reading mat."
Direction:	"Line up quickly and quietly."
Positive repetition:	"Debbie is in line. That was very fast! Richard is in his place, too."
Direction:	"Eyes on me and no talking, please."
Positive repetition:	"Jeff, thank you for having your eyes on me. Brian is sitting quietly."

A note to teachers of older students: With adolescents, such overt positive recognition in front of their peers can backfire. Nothing is more embarrassing for many adolescents than to be singled out for being "good" in the classroom. One way around this dilemma is for you to pair your positive statement with an action that benefits the entire class. Thus we come to the concept of combining positive repetition with a classwide positive support system.

A classwide positive support system is typically a point system that enables the entire class to earn a reward they want, for example, free homework night or free time. This concept will be discussed in detail later in this chapter (pages 155-156).

Here's an example of an eighth-grade teacher who's using a classwide support system to help teach her students to go to their cooperative learning groups.

"When you go to your small groups, I want you to take your assignment, walk quietly, sit down with your group and start your assignment.

"Marco's walking quietly. Yumi has her assignment. She's seated and ready to go. That's a point for the class toward free time. We have 18 points. Two more and you get a homework-free night."

Harness the power that's in your classroom! Peer pressure is a very compelling force, particularly with older students. It's already there, so use it to your advantage.

If this continual attention to positive repetition seems time consuming, just remember that at the beginning of the year you're setting in motion a classroom environment based on recognition, caring and positive support. To create this environment you will need to work harder at it in the early stages.

Also keep in mind that you may be new to implementing positive support in this manner. Practice makes perfect! The more accustomed you become to integrating positive repetition into your teaching flow, the more comfortable you'll be using it.

In Chapter 13, Pulling It All Together, you will see some helpful examples of teachers who teach subject matter, give praise and motivate students all at the same time.

How often should you use positive repetition?

At the beginning of the year you will be placing a heavy emphasis on teaching students how to behave. The more you want to teach children how to behave, the more you need to use praise. Thus, at the beginning of the year you will use positive repetition much more frequently than you will once your students learn what you need them to do in each classroom situation.

Remember, the goal of positive reinforcement is to start strong, then gradually decrease its frequency.

Guidelines for Frequency of Positive Repetition

Weeks 1-2	Use positive repetition every time you give a direction. Don't worry about overdoing it.
Weeks 2-4	Use positive repetition every third time you give a direction.
After first month	Use positive repetition every fourth time you give a direction. Maintain this frequency level throughout the year.

Remember our goal to praise each student every day?

Positive repetition can help you reach this goal, easily and without a lot of extra thought. Think of it this way: You may give 100 directions a day. If, with every fourth direction you give, you praise a student—that's 25 times a day you'll be praising kids. Through positive repetition alone you can praise every student every day.

How to Keep Students On Task

You've learned how positive repetition can motivate students to follow directions and get on task. Now, what can you do to *keep* them on task?

The best way to build responsible student behavior is to continually provide frequent positive recognition to those students who are on task.

Let students know that you notice and appreciate their good work. Give them the encouragement they need to keep it up.

Here are some techniques that will motivate students to continue their appropriate behavior and, at the same time, motivate those students who need some behavior reminders.

Consistent Praise

An effective way to encourage students' appropriate behavior is to continually monitor the class—even while teaching—and provide frequent praise and positive support to those students who are on task.

Always keep in mind that you are not only teaching students reading, writing, or math, but you are also teaching them how to behave in a manner that will maximize their learning. Here's an example of a teacher using consistent praise integrated with teaching a lesson:

Teacher: Now let's practice our multiplication tables. How much is seven times three? I am looking for students with their hands up and waiting to be called upon.

(Many students raise their hands. Several mumble or shout out answers. The teacher focuses on Kelly who has her hand raised and is not speaking.)

Teacher: Kelly, thank you for raising your hand and waiting quietly. What's the answer?

(The teacher praises the student and restates the appropriate behavior.)

Kelly: Twenty-one.

Teacher: That's excellent! Next, seven times five?

(The teacher again watches for students who have their hands raised and are not speaking out.)

Teacher: Yes, Robert?

Robert: Thirty-four.

Teacher: Good try. That's almost right, Robert! Thank you for raising your hand and waiting for me to call on you. Now, would anyone else like to try seven times five? Chris, you have your hand up. What's the answer?

Chris: Thirty-five.

Teacher: Great work, Chris. And I see that most of you are remembering to raise your hands and waiting to be called upon before you answer.

You can see in this example that the teacher was doing more than just teaching multiplication. She was also teaching students how to raise their hands and wait to be called upon before speaking (her specific direction for this activity). By integrating behavior management into her teaching routine, this teacher will ensure that her lessons are more productive for both her and her students.

Guidelines for Using Praise

To make the praise you give as effective as possible, keep these guidelines in mind:

- Effective praise is personal.

When you offer praise, always include the student's name. Let students know, "These words are directed to *you*. Thanks for your great effort!"

This is especially important when you are praising the behavior of a student who is across the room. A statement such as, "Thank you for working quietly back there," is not as effective as, "Jack and Sally are working quietly. Thank you."

- Effective praise must be genuine.

To be convincing to students, to show that you really mean what you say, be genuinely appreciative of their appropriate behavior. Insincere or mechanical praise, praise that's given by the clock, not by the situation, is no praise at all.

- Effective praise is descriptive and specific.

Descriptive praise reinforces the desired behavior by mentioning it: "Beth is walking quietly in line. Good job, Beth." "You went right to work, Simon. Terrific!" Specific praise lets the student know when he or she is behaving appropriately, and increases the likelihood that the behavior will be repeated. Avoid evaluative comments such as "I like the way you are working." They're not as effective as descriptive, specific statements because the student is focusing on whether the teacher likes him rather than on what he is doing correctly.

Descriptive Praise	Vague Praise
"Sue is lined up ready for recess. Thanks, Sue."	"Way to go, Sue."
"You did a great job outlining your essay, Robin."	"Nice job, Robin."
"Thank you for putting the books away, Kerry."	"I like the way you're helping, Kerry."

• Effective praise is age-appropriate.

You cannot praise a kindergarten student the same way you would a high school student. Here are some guidelines:

Grades K-3: Young children want your approval publicly. It means a lot to them to know that you approve of their actions. Thus, your positive statements to your students should reflect the fact that you, their teacher, noticed the good behavior.

> "I see you went all morning without talking out. That's really impressive, Kirby!"

> "Jessica, you put a lot of work into your science project. The posters you painted are so interesting. I love them!"

Grades 4-6: As students mature, your approval of their actions is still important, but it becomes more important that they feel good about themselves. Your praise needs to reflect this shift in attitude.

> "You went all morning without shouting out. You should be proud of yourself."

> "Earl, your science project reflects a lot of research on your part. All your work paid off. This is an excellent presentation!"

Grades 7-12: The key to making effective positive comments to adolescents is to do it in a simple, matter-of-fact manner to the student. The more simple and direct, the better. Your praise may also be more appreciated by older students if it is given privately, and not in front of the entire class.

> "You were quiet all period, Scott. Thank you."

> "Excellent project, Kim. It gave me a lot to think about."

Make praise the most consistent positive reinforcement technique you use. Start thinking now about all the opportunities you have each day to recognize your students' successes.

Scanning

A common behavior problem, particularly at the beginning of the year, is keeping students working independently.

The scanning technique is useful when you are working with a small group of students, or an individual student, while the rest of the class is working independently. The objective of this technique is to reinforce students who are on task, thereby encouraging them to remain on task. This technique will help you recognize students who may normally not receive attention until they misbehave.

By using this technique, you can keep independent workers on task and still remain working with one small group.

Here's how to use the scanning technique:

When you are working with a small group, look up every few minutes and scan the students who are working independently. As you notice students who are working appropriately, take a moment to recognize their good behavior.

> "David is working quietly on his math. Thank you, David."

The student will appreciate the recognition and continue working independently. Other students will get the message that you are aware of what's going on in the room, and will be motivated to stay on task themselves.

Here's an example of how scanning is used when a teacher is working with a small reading group and the rest of the class is working independently.

Teacher: All right, Doug. Please read from the top of page eighty-three.

(Doug reads the paragraph.)

Teacher: Doug, excellent job. You read with such feeling!

(The teacher looks up, scans the class and sees that Jack is busily at work on his assignment. She takes the opportunity to recognize his effort.)

Teacher: Jack, it looks like you're working hard on your report.

(Jack looks up, smiles, and continues his work. Other students look up also, and then focus back on their assignments.)

How often you use the scanning technique will depend on your students' age and level of motivation. At the beginning of the year remind students of expected behavior by using praise with scanning often. Later during the year you may not want to interrupt on-task behavior with even a positive statement. But no matter how you use this technique, scanning demonstrates to students that you are always aware of their appropriate behavior, even when you are not working directly with them.

Guidelines for using the scanning technique:

Week 1	Scan the classroom every 3-4 minutes.
Weeks 2-4	Scan the classroom every 5-10 minutes.
After first month	Use this technique as needed.

Circulating the Classroom.

While students are working independently, circulate throughout the room and give positive recognition. One-on-one, you can always let a student know that you recognize his or her appropriate behavior. This is a particularly effective technique to use with secondary students.

> "Mike, you are doing a great job on your work. You finished the entire assignment!"

You may also want to give a student general praise for how she is behaving.

> "Kim, you are very cooperative today. You are doing a wonderful job getting along with everyone."

Circulating among your students also lets them know that you're reachable. You're there, available to give help when needed.

There is no need to phase out this technique. Keep it going strong all year long. Each time you circulate the classroom you have an opportunity to show your students you care, and that you notice their good efforts.

Don't stay seated behind your desk.

Use independent work time as a time to move among your students, be available for questions, and boost students' self-esteem through praise and positive support. This is an opportunity for teachers at all grade levels to let their students know that they recognize something special about them.

As any upper-grade teacher knows, providing consistent and meaningful positive recognition to adolescents can be a challenge. Here's how one 10th-grade social studies teacher overcame the challenge. He calls his technique "working the room."

"Whenever my students are working independently, whether alone or in groups, I take the opportunity to do some 'esteem boosting.' While the kids are busy, I don't sit down and I don't grade papers. As they work, I roam around the classroom. I might stop by one student's desk, lean down and quietly praise his work.

"To another student I might mention what a good-looking shirt he has on. To still another I might jot a quick positive note for her to take home to parents.

"The point is, I stay in touch with a word, a smile, a personal comment. Working the room helps keep the students on task and it gives me an opportunity for some one-to-one contact.

"In ten minutes I can let six to ten students know that I care about them—unobtrusively and naturally."

Names on the Board for Good Behavior

Highlight students who are behaving. It's a great way to back up the praise you give.

A motivating way to encourage younger students is to simply write their names on the board when you catch them being good. Designate a corner of the blackboard as Classroom Superstars Corner. Play a game of, "How many names can we get on the board today!" Set a goal to put at least 20 names on the board each day.

Erase the names at the end of the day and start fresh the next day.

Implementing Classwide Reward Systems

In this chapter we've talked about using praise to motivate students to behave appropriately. Now let's talk about how classwide recognition systems can augment your positive reinforcement efforts as well.

When we think about classwide rewards, our thoughts often go to a first-grade teacher we worked with a number of years ago. She was the consummate master at using Marbles in a Jar (see page 74) to motivate students! She used this classwide reward system to help teach students her behavioral expectations at the beginning of the year, and she used it throughout the year when students needed some "following directions" reminders.

On the first day of school she always had marbles and a jar close at hand and ready to use. Her goal was to use the marbles continually to reinforce the students for following directions. She always set an easy goal for the students to reach at first. Thirty marbles in the jar would typically earn the class free time. And within the first day she would see to it that the students would earn the free time. More important was the combination of the "clink" of the marbles with the words of praise, "Good job following directions." Her students were learning in a positive and quick manner how to follow her directions.

After a few days she increased the number of marbles needed to earn the free time. By the end of the second week of school, the marbles were no longer needed. The students had learned to follow directions and quickly get on task and stay on task.

Throughout the year, whenever a problem developed, the marbles reappeared.

This classwide recognition system was particularly helpful on "high disruption" days such as the first snowfall and the first day back to school after winter vacation.

By using the Marbles in a Jar technique this teacher was able to encourage students to behave responsibly and appropriately in a positive and enjoyable manner, without having to rely on threats or consequences to motivate her students to behave.

Here's another example of a classwide reward system in action.

A middle-school English teacher we know had a very active, very social seventh-grade class. These students always seemed to prefer clowning around to settling down to work.

Praising students who were on task, even one-to-one, proved ineffective. He found he was having to provide consequences to more and more students and the classroom was becoming an increasingly negative environment for all.

To counteract this, he instituted a classwide recognition system. Whenever he caught a student on task, that student earned a point for the entire class. Fifty points would earn a night of no homework. The students quickly became motivated to reach the goal, and could often be heard making comments like "Shhhh, cool it, be quiet!" Within a week, the points were earned. The teacher kept the point system in place for the next three weeks. By the end of this time period, the socialization had subsided, the classroom environment was more positive and learning had increased.

This is a particularly advantageous technique to use with older students because rather than the teacher having to control the students' behavior, the students are motivated to employ peer pressure to monitor themselves.

How to Increase Your Consistency in Giving Positive Recognition

It's not easy to maintain a high frequency of praise and positive recognition in the classroom. Most of us don't do it naturally. With this in mind, we want to share some highly effective techniques that will help ensure more frequent positive reinforcement.

Have a P. R. (Positive Reminder) Plan.

Don't let positive recognition slip your mind even for a moment! These ideas will keep a positive word right on the tip of your tongue all day long.

1. Post classroom reminders.

   How many times a day do you glance at the classroom clock? Now you can get more than just the time of day when you look at the clock. Hang a "Catch 'em being good" reminder on the wall right next to the clock. This timely note will give you a nudge throughout the day, and remind you to keep looking for positive behavior to reinforce.

2. Put reminders in lesson plans.

   Your lesson-plan book is a great place to jot down reminders to yourself. Make a note that in addition to teaching subject matter, you will also praise students for appropriate behavior. Write in fluorescent marking pen to really highlight the idea!

3. Set specific goals for the frequency of your praise and positive recognition.

   Goals help give direction and structure to our efforts. Each day in your lesson-plan book write your goals for delivering praise and positive reinforcement.

   "I will write 20 students' names on the board for behaving appropriately."

"I will send home 2 positive notes per day per class."

"Each class will earn 10 classwide points per period."

Positive recognition and support results in students feeling good about themselves. When students feel good about themselves, when they feel confident about what they are doing, their self-esteem rises and they are motivated to behave better and achieve academically.

With the consistent use of praise and positive support, you can take a major step in ensuring your students' success in your classroom.

As you go through the school day, always keep in mind that the goal of a successful teacher is to recognize the appropriate behavior of every student at least one time a day. All students should go home every night feeling good about something they have done, believing that you really do care, and knowing that you really are there for them.

CHAPTER TEN — KEY POINTS

Using Positive Recognition to Motivate Students to Behave

- Use positive repetition to reinforce students who are following directions, and to give a positively stated reminder to those students who are not yet following the directions.

- Integrate consistent praise into any lesson or any interaction with students.

- Use the scanning technique when you are working with a small group of students and the rest of the class is working independently.

- As you teach, circulate throughout the classroom and keep giving praise.

- Recognize younger students for good behavior by writing their names on the board as a Classroom Superstar!

- Use positive support to encourage students to continue appropriate behavior.

- Use positive support to increase a student's self-esteem.

- Use positive support to reduce behavior problems.

- Consistent positive support will create a more positive classroom environment for you and your students.

- Make a goal to praise every student every day.

- Use a classwide recognition system to motivate your class to work toward a specific behavioral goal.

TEACHING RESPONSIBLE BEHAVIOR

Part 3: Redirecting Non-Disruptive Off-Task Behavior

By teaching your rules and specific directions, and by providing consistent positive recognition to your students, you are going to eliminate the vast majority of problems before they begin.

But let's be realistic. No matter how clearly you teach your expectations, and no matter how positive you are, there will still be students who engage in behavior that is not in their best interest—behavior that doesn't enhance their self-esteem, doesn't promote their success in school and behavior that frustrates you or causes you to feel stressed at the end of the day.

This behavior can take two forms: disruptive off-task behavior and non-disruptive off-task behavior.

Disruptive off-task behavior means a student is keeping you from teaching or other students from learning. Because it is so obtrusive, disruptive behavior is easy to recognize. We will be looking at how to deal with this behavior in Chapter 12.

Disruptive Off-Task Behaviors:

> Shouting out in class
>
> Throwing paper airplanes
>
> Pushing or shoving another student
>
> Running in the classroom
>
> Talking back

Non-disruptive off-task behavior, on the other hand, is not always as easy to identify or respond to.

Non-Disruptive Off-Task Behaviors:

> Looking out the window
>
> Reading instead of listening
>
> Doodling instead of working
>
> Working on an assignment from another class
>
> Daydreaming or sleeping with head down on arms

Non-disruptive off-task behavior means a student is not disturbing others, but he's not paying attention or following directions either. He's physically in the classroom, but attentively, the seat is vacant.

Welcome to the gray zone of behavior management: Your classroom appears to be running smoothly. No one's disrupting, except you notice one of your students isn't really participating. He's sitting there quietly, but he's looking out the window, or his head is down on his desk.

What can be done to lead this student back into classroom activity, or should you do anything?

It's always surprising to go into a classroom and see a teacher lecturing or giving instructions while some students are obviously paying no attention.

These teachers are ignoring the inappropriate behavior. It may be unintentional, but these teachers are, in effect, condoning and allowing behavior that is not in their students' best interests. They're telling their students, "In my class it's OK to not pay attention; it's OK to look out the window while I'm speaking. In my class it's OK not to learn."

Non-disruptive off-task behavior hurts the students engaged in that behavior. As a professional, it's your job and your responsibility to teach each student. Non-disruptive off-task behavior is unacceptable and must be dealt with correctly.

But how?

Here's how many teachers typically deal with non-disruptive off-task behavior:

1. They ignore the problem.

2. They give an immediate, sometimes harsh, consequence.

Let's look at the effect each of these responses has on the situation.

Ignoring the problem:

When a teacher ignores non-disruptive off-task behavior, it's like giving the student license to not learn. Don't let these students become shadows in your classroom.

Take the time to keep them involved and attentive in your classroom. Make the effort to get them interested in your lessons and keep them interested. Students depend on your caring enough to teach them, to educate them.

Issuing an immediate consequence:

You're teaching a lesson. Everything seems to be going along fine. Students are quiet and seem to be paying attention—until you look out and see Jason rocking back and forth in his chair, staring out the window. Instant reaction: "Jason, sit up and listen! You've just lost recess today!"

Recognize non-disruptive off-task behavior for what it is: a lapse of attention. It needs to be corrected calmly, with care and understanding.

Controlling your students' non-disruptive off-task behavior with immediate consequences is not the answer, and many times alienates potentially enthusiastic students.

Redirect Students Back on Task

The teachers who deal most successfully with non-disruptive off-task behavior do so with a variety of techniques which are woven into their style of teaching.

In a manner that neither stops them from teaching or raises their stress level, they remain in control and continue with their lesson plans. They never miss a beat. There's no alarm in their voice or anger in their response.

Here are four techniques used to redirect non-disruptive off-task behavior.

Redirecting Technique #1: The "Look"

Communicate that you are aware of and disapprove of the behavior.

Giving a look that says, "I'm aware of and disapprove of your behavior" is an effective way of redirecting non-disruptive off-task behavior.

> Instead of doing his assignment, Devon sits rocking back and forth in his chair. Noticing Devon's off-task behavior, the teacher makes direct eye contact with him, and looks straight at him with a firm, calm look on her face. She maintains eye contact until he puts all four legs of his chair on the floor and gets back to his assignment.

The teacher made eye contact. She gave a look that clearly said, "I am aware of and disapprove of your behavior, Devon." Devon got back on task.

Redirecting Technique #2: Physical Proximity

Stand by the student's side.

Use this technique as a natural part of your teaching strategy. Redirect a student back on task by simply walking over and standing close by. The student will know why you've arrived at his side and he will respond. Not a word or a thought is dropped from your lessons.

> While lecturing, the teacher notices that Shannon put her head down and "tuned out." Continuing to lecture, the teacher walks to the back of the room to Shannon's seat and stands near her desk while continuing to instruct the class.

With this action the teacher clearly and firmly communicated to the student that his behavior was inappropriate.

Redirecting Technique #3: Mention the off-task student's name while teaching.

Say the student's name.

Just mentioning a student's name while you are teaching a lesson may be enough to redirect his attention back on task.

> While at the board, the teacher notices that Tanya and Michael are off task and not paying attention. The teacher, in a matter-of-fact manner, continues the lesson saying, "I want all of you, including Tanya and Michael, to come up with the answer to this problem." As soon as their names are mentioned, Tanya and Michael immediately begin paying attention.

Redirecting Technique #4: Proximity Praise

Accentuate the positive.

Another way to redirect a student back on task is to focus on the appropriate behavior of those students around him.

> The entire class, with the exception of John, is working on their assignments. On either side of John, James and Cindy are both following directions and doing their work. Wanting to get John on task, the teacher says, "James and Cindy are doing an excellent job on their assignments."
>
> As she expects, John looks around him, notices what is going on and gets back to work.

What the teacher was saying to John in a supportive way was, "I'm aware that you're not doing your work, John, and I want you back on task." At the same time, she was giving verbal praise to those students who were on task.

Each of the four redirecting techniques presented here are easy to use and do not interrupt the flow of your teaching. Using these techniques results in a winning situation for everyone: You can keep teaching and the off-task student resumes learning. You prevent potentially disruptive behavior before it begins.

Once a student is back on track?

Recognize the student's appropriate behavior. As soon as a student is back on task, take advantage of the opportunity to praise his behavior.

When is enough enough?

By now you may be saying to yourself, "It all sounds easy here on the pages of a book, but in my class some of those off-task students will go right back off task a few minutes later. How many times do I redirect them before I start giving consequences?

That's an important question. Redirecting off-task behavior is a good technique that gives students an opportunity to get back to work. But you can't bend over backward, either. Non-disruptive off-task behavior can't be allowed to go on continuously or it becomes disruptive behavior.

You want to prevent disruptive behavior. You cannot allow the student to get into a pattern of failure.

Note: If the behavior seems out of character for that student, perhaps there's something wrong. Check it out. Talk to the student after class and ask, "Is there something I can do? Let's talk." Always remember that your own good judgment is your most valuable tool in assessing student behavior.

Here's a rule of thumb:

When you find yourself having to redirect a student three times a day (elementary) or two times a class period (secondary), you can assume that the student is not receiving enough structure to help him control his behavior. In these situations, turn to your disciplinary hierarchy and issue a warning.

If the off-task behavior continues, you may need to use consequences from your disciplinary hierarchy (to be covered in Chapter 12, Implementing Consequences).

CHAPTER ELEVEN — KEY POINTS

Redirecting Non-Disruptive Off-Task Behavior

- Differentiate between disruptive behavior and non-disruptive off-task behavior. Non-disruptive off-task behavior is behavior in which a student is not disturbing others, but is not paying attention or following directions either.

- Don't ignore non-disruptive off-task behavior. It's not in your students' best interest.

- Rather than provide a consequence, or ignore the behavior, redirect the behavior.

- Redirect a student's non-disruptive off-task behavior while you continue teaching.

- Give the student a "look" that says you are aware of and disapprove of his behavior.

- Stand by an off-task student's side as you teach.

- Mention the off-task student's name while teaching.

- Use proximity praise to redirect an off-task student.

- As soon as a student is back on task, take the first opportunity to praise his appropriate behavior.

- If redirecting is not effective it may be appropriate to provide consequences from your discipline hierarchy.

CHAPTER TWELVE

IMPLEMENTING CONSEQUENCES

Simply planning consequences and teaching them to your students is not going to be sufficient to motivate all students to behave. You are going to have to follow through when they disrupt.

Remember, actions speak louder than words.

In Chapter 7 you learned to develop a discipline hierarchy as part of your classroom discipline plan. How you use the consequences in the hierarchy will determine its success in helping you motivate students to choose responsible behavior.

Students need to learn that negative consequences are a natural outcome of misbehavior.

The key is not the consequences themselves, but the inevitability that they will occur each time a rule is broken or a direction is not followed. Not sometimes. Not every now and then, but every single time.

Consequences given consistently and calmly help teach students to behave responsibly. The consistent use of consequences teaches students that if they choose to behave in an inappropriate manner, they will also choose to accept the negative consequences of that choice.

To successfully manage a classroom, there must be a balance between positive support and limit-setting consequences.

Students will not respect your praise unless it is backed up with firm limits—and limits will be ineffective unless staying within those limits is backed up by praise.

Guidelines for Using Consequences

Here are the basic guidelines to follow to ensure that your use of disciplinary consequences will help students choose responsible behavior.

1. Provide consequences in a calm, matter-of-fact manner.

How you provide consequences to students is as important as the consequences themselves. All too many teachers get frustrated and angry when students disrupt, and their responses reflect this frustration.

Here's an example of this frustration:

> In a seventh-grade class, Kirk and Stephen begin talking and laughing while a study team is giving a group report. Kirk and Stephen receive a warning. As the study team resumes the presentation, Kirk and Stephen once again begin disrupting.

Teacher: *(angry tone of voice)* Kirk, Stephen, there you go again being rude and inconsiderate. I've had it with your immature behavior. You can just cut it out right now. I'll see you both after class!

Stay calm. Getting angry and demeaning students is counterproductive. All you need to point out to students who are disruptive is what they should be doing and the consequence they will receive.

Here's how that situation should have been handled:

Teacher: *(calmly)* Kirk and Stephen, this is not the time to be talking and laughing. You need to be listening. You have chosen to stay after class.

2. Be consistent. Provide a consequence every time students choose to disrupt.

Here's an example of consistency in action:

> Students in a sixth-grade class are working independently. One student, Jean, turns around and starts scribbling on Bert's paper. Bert says, "Stop it, Jean. Leave me alone!"
>
> The teacher walks up to Jean's desk and says, "Jean, you know that you are not to write on someone else's paper. I want you to turn around and do your work. That's a warning."
>
> The teacher writes Jean's name on his clipboard and stands right by to redirect her back to work.
>
> A few minutes later, Jean turns around and this time tries to grab Bert's paper. The teacher again walks up to Jean. "Jean, you're obviously having a hard time doing your work without bothering your neighbors. Will you please take your work and go sit in the back of the class for the next five minutes? After class, I want you to fill out the behavior journal and think about what you should have been doing rather than bothering your neighbor."
>
> The teacher puts a check by Jean's name.

When we consider the issue of consistency, we are reminded of an eighth-grade math class that was so disruptive their teacher quit midway through the semester. When the new teacher arrived, she encountered constant disruptions as students talked back, shouted out, left their seats and behaved belligerently.

> On her first day the new teacher explained her rules to the students. She told them what would happen when they followed the rules, and the consequences they would receive if they chose not to behave appropriately. The

students in turn virtually ignored the rules. The teacher attempted to recognize those few students who were on task, but her comments fell on deaf ears.

She then began to give consequences from her discipline plan. Each time a student broke a classroom rule, she gave a consequence. The students thought it was a joke and some tried to get as many checks as they could. By the end of the period that first day, nine students had reached the fourth step on the hierarchy, which meant that their parents were to be called. As she excused the students, the teacher clearly announced that she was going to be speaking to a number of parents that evening. One particularly belligerent young man responded, "No way any teacher is going to call all those parents!"

The next day in class the students compared notes and found out the teacher had meant what she had said. All the parents had been called. That same day four students reached the fourth level of the hierarchy. That night the teacher called their parents.

Over the next several weeks, the students periodically challenged her. They soon realized that every time a student disrupted there would be a consequence. As the days went by, the students' respect for their new teacher grew. They began to place more value on her positive comments and recognition than on attracting her attention through disruptions. Her praise and support replaced the consequences. And learning replaced the chaos that had once existed in the classroom.

As this teacher said, "I never in my life had to be so firm and so consistent when dealing with my students." It was the students' behavior that told her she needed to set limits, and stick with those limits.

3. After a student receives a consequence, find the first opportunity you can to recognize positive behavior.

Here's a common problem many teachers share: After a student has been disruptive, after he or she has received a consequence, all the teacher does is focus on that student's negative behavior. The teacher is angry at the student and is just looking for an opportunity to catch him or her disrupting again.

Don't fall into this trap. Instead, take the first opportunity to recognize the student's appropriate behavior. You may have to provide another consequence if the student continues to disrupt, but try to diffuse the tension by finding something positive to say.

If you want to reduce your own stress and tension level, look for something positive the student is doing and praise him for it!

Let's return to the example of Kirk and Stephen. In the past scenario, each of the boys had received a check and therefore were to stay after school:

Kirk and Stephen are now working quietly, participating appropriately in their group. The teacher walks up to both of them.

> Teacher: Kirk, Stephen, you both are working quietly, and you're both doing a good job helping out the whole group. You are making much better choices about how to behave.

It should always be your goal to teach students that you are more interested in focusing on their appropriate behavior than their inappropriate actions.

4. Provide an "escape mechanism" for students who are upset and want to talk about what happened.

Many times after receiving a consequence, students will want you to stop what you are doing and listen to their side of the story. Most of the time you will not be able to stop your lesson at that moment to listen to their concerns. You do want to let the students know that you do care about what they have to say. In this situation, many teachers use an "escape mechanism" that allows students to diffuse their anger and "get something off their chest," without disrupting the rest of the class. Escape mechanisms can include:

- Having the student write you a note that you will discuss with him or her after class or when you have a break in the lesson.

- Using a notebook to record misbehavior that allows space for students to write their comments.

- Having students keep a daily journal or diary in which they can record any comments.

If you use an escape mechanism, remember that it is not a substitute for talking with the student about improved behavior. It is simply a tool that allows you to deal with a student's anger or frustration in a way that does not disrupt classroom instruction.

5. When a student continuously disrupts, "move in."

There may be times when a student will continue to disrupt even after he or she is given a warning or a consequence. All too often when this occurs, a teacher will get angry and continue to give the student one consequence after another until the student ends up being sent out of the classroom. This drastic reaction may not be in the student's best interest.

Here's what we mean:

Darcy, a sixth-grade student, has just received a warning and a check.

Darcy:	Oh, c'mon, man. Just get off my case.
Teacher:	*(getting angry)* I'm sick of your attitude, Darcy. You say one more word and it's another check.
Darcy:	I don't care. Give me another check.

Teacher:	*(getting angrier)* OK, now that's two checks. I'm not taking this from you, young lady.
Darcy:	Give me another check. See if I care. Go on.
Teacher:	Darcy, one more word and you're out of here.
Darcy:	Word.
Teacher:	That's it. Get out.

What happened here? This situation clearly got out of hand. How could you handle it more effectively?

Before something like this occurs, before you and the student both get angry, take control of the situation. Diffuse the anger by talking one-to-one with the student.

Use the "moving in" technique:

- Move close to the student.

  Walk up to the student. Get close. Show your concern and in a quiet, firm manner let the student know that his or her behavior is inappropriate.

- Remind the student of the consequences received so far, and what will happen next if the misbehavior continues.

The key to handling this technique successfully is your confident, firm manner. Let's take a look now at how Darcy could have been dealt with using the moving in technique.

Darcy has just received a warning and a consequence.

Darcy:	Oh, c'mon, man. Just get off my case.
Teacher:	*(walks up to Darcy's desk. Leans down and speaks in a caring, yet firm tone.)*
	Darcy, I'm concerned that your behavior is going to result in some consequences that you don't really want. You've been doing well in

this class lately, and I'd like to see that continue. You and I both know that you've been trying and succeeding in your work.

Now, you've received a warning and a consequence. One more inappropriate comment and you'll stay behind two minutes after the other students leave. Do you understand?

Many times, physical proximity is all that is needed to help calm a student down and stop the disruptive behavior. Walk up to the student. Show your concern. Let the student know that the behavior is inappropriate. Let the student know that you care.

With older students, "move out."

With older students, it may be more appropriate to "move out" of the classroom to speak to the student. Removing the audience of peers may increase the effectiveness of your limit-setting efforts.

When you "move out," remember to:

- stay calm.

- avoid arguing with the student.

- recognize the student's feelings.

In the previous example, if the student were older, the teacher would have moved her outside the classroom to continue the conversation.

When Students Challenge Your Authority

By providing consequences calmly and consistently, you will effectively help most students choose responsible behavior, and stop most disruptive behavior in your classroom.

But in spite of these efforts, there are going to be some cases in which students will challenge your authority and confront you. These confrontations can take various forms—anger, tears, even tantrums. But whatever the form, all are designed to hook you emotionally, escalate the situation and get you to back down from the limits you have set.

Refocus an argumentative conversation.

Keep this in mind: When a student tries to manipulate you or argue with you, you must stay in charge and *refocus* the conversation. Do not get involved in an argument. Do not let the student pull you into a pointless exchange.

Instead,

- Stay calm.

- State what you want: "I want you to sit down and complete your assignment."

- Preface your statement of want with understanding for the child.

- Repeat your statement of want a maximum of three times. If the student still argues, let him know that he may be choosing to receive a consequence.

For example:

Teacher:	Tom, I want you to sit down and get to work on your assignment.
Tom:	Why are you picking on me? Cynthia's not doing her work. She's just playing around, too.
Teacher:	I understand, Tom, but I want you to sit down and start your work.
Tom:	But why do I have to if Cynthia doesn't?
Teacher:	Tom, I see you're upset, but sit down and begin your work.

Tom:	But I see lots of kids who aren't doing anything.
Teacher:	Tom, if you do not get to work immediately, you and I will call your father during recess. The choice is yours.

Note: This refocusing technique should only be used to diffuse a student's anger—when a student is trying to manipulate a situation in a way that is not in his best interest. This technique is not meant to be used as a means to cut off communication.

Let's look now at some disruptive situations and see how they can be handled both ineffectively and effectively.

Dealing with Crying or Tantrums

Sometimes young students become upset when given a consequence. Many have learned that by crying they can get their way, and they will attempt to see if it works with you. Here is an example:

Teacher:	Maria, I cannot allow you to push another student. Please go and sit by yourself in the time-out area.
Maria:	*(starting to cry)* I didn't mean to.
Teacher:	Now, Maria, just relax. There's no need to cry every time I talk to you.
Maria:	*(sobbing harder)* But I didn't do anything. I only tapped her.
Teacher:	Maria, just calm down. Please. I'm not angry with you. Calm down. You don't have to sit by yourself. Just blow your nose and settle down.

If a child's tears are out of character, you need to find out what is going on. But for many children, tears are part of a pattern of behavior that enables them to manipulate adults and get their way.

Now let's look at how a teacher could more effectively have dealt with Maria:

Teacher: Maria, I cannot allow you to push another student. Please go and sit by yourself in the time-out area.

Maria: *(starting to cry)* I didn't do anything.

Teacher: Maria, I can see you are really upset. I can see you do not want to sit by yourself. But you chose to push Samantha and therefore you've chosen to sit by yourself.

Maria: *(crying harder)* But I didn't do anything. I only tapped her.

Teacher: Maria, I hear what you are saying. Now, please go sit in the time-out area. When you are calmer I will call you back to the group.

The teacher was empathetic but firm. She listened to the student and showed her that she understood her feelings. Yet she still stood her ground. She let the student know that the consequence stands, in spite of the tears.

Dealing with Covert Anger

Middle and secondary students sometimes will attempt to hook you emotionally by giving looks of defiance, by slamming books or by mumbling under their breath. Actions such as these tend to trigger reactive responses from teachers.

Teacher: Toni, I told you to cut it out. Stop playing with your makeup and take out your book and get to work.

(Toni slowly takes out her book while glaring at the teacher.)

Teacher: *(angrily)* What's your problem, Toni? Don't look at me like that, young lady.

Toni: *(rudely)* I'm not looking at you.

Teacher: I'm tired of that attitude, young lady.

Toni: Likewise.

This situation is going to go nowhere. The student hooked the teacher with a dirty look and a confrontation ensued that neither can win.

Whenever possible, simply ignore the covert hostility of a student. By ignoring the behavior you will diffuse the situation. Remember, what you really want is for the student to comply with your request. Whether or not the student does it in an angry manner is not the issue. The student is still complying with your expectations. Many students need the "angry out" to save face.

Here's a better approach to the same situation:

Teacher: Toni, the direction was to do your work, not put on makeup. Now please take out your book. That's a check.

(Toni takes out her book while glaring at the teacher. Seeing that Toni is getting to work, the teacher calmly distances herself from her. Later, as Toni leaves the class, the teacher takes her aside and thanks her for getting to work.)

By ignoring the angry look, the teacher diffused the confrontation. It didn't get out of hand, and the student resumed her work.

Overt Anger

Some students, especially those who want control, will provoke angry confrontations with a teacher to get their way. It is critical in dealing with such a student that you remain calm and distance yourself from the anger of the student. Most teachers, however, get hooked by the student's anger.

Here's what we mean:

Sheila is reading a magazine while she is in her learning group. The other students keep asking her to participate, but she angrily refuses and taunts them for doing their work.

Teacher:	What's the problem?
Student:	We need Sheila's help. She just keeps bothering us and won't do anything.
Teacher:	Sheila, what's going on? Is there something I can do to help you get started?
Sheila:	These guys are all nerds. I'm not doing this stupid assignment.
Teacher:	Sheila, watch your mouth!
Sheila:	I can talk any way I want. I don't have to listen to you.
Teacher:	*(upset)* Sheila, yes you do. I am tired of you mouthing off at me and the other kids.
Sheila:	Well, I'm tired of you, too.
Teacher:	You'll be sorry you ever said that, young lady.
Sheila:	Yeah? What are you going to do? You're a joke. You are just a joke.

This teacher got hooked by Sheila's anger and lost control.

Here are a few guidelines for handling a student's overt anger more successfully.

> **First, use what we call a *paradoxical response.*** The more upset the student becomes, the calmer you must become. The calmer you are, the more it will diffuse the student's anger. Keep in mind that the student may be accustomed to parents or teachers becoming upset or angry when they

get angry. When the teacher stays calm, the student may not know how to react.

Next, move the student away from other students.
Students who are angry want an audience. The audience feeds their emotions. Moving the student away can further diffuse the situation.

Here's how the situation could have been handled:

Teacher:	What's the problem?
Students:	We need Sheila's help. She just keeps bothering us and won't do anything.
Teacher:	Sheila, what's going on? Can't you work with your group?
Sheila:	These guys are all nerds. I'm not doing this stupid assignment.
Teacher:	I can see you're upset, but I can't allow you to talk that way in class.
Sheila:	I can talk any way I want. I don't have to listen to you.
Teacher:	*(calmly)* Sheila, please come outside with me. We need to talk about this. I cannot allow you to talk this way in class.
Sheila:	No!
Teacher:	Sheila, you have a choice. Either come outside with me or you'll have to go to Mr. Boyer's office.
Sheila:	I don't care. Send me.
Teacher:	I'm sorry you made that choice. You need to go to the office now. I want to talk to you about this later so we can work this out.

The teacher remained calm and firm, and communicated to the student she was concerned about her.

Now what do you do if the student refuses to leave? It does no good to argue with the student and keep telling her to leave and have her say no to you. You will need to summon assistance.

You will need to have the backup of a discipline team. A discipline team is made up of administrators and/or other teachers or staff at the school. You need to contact the office when you have a problem you cannot deal with. The team comes to your classroom and assists you with the student.

Back to the example of Sheila:

Let's see how the teacher could have successfully dealt with the situation if Sheila had refused to leave.

> Sheila: I'm not leaving. I won't go.
>
> Teacher: *(calmly)* Sheila, I cannot make you leave, but I will call the office and have someone escort you out.
>
> Sheila: I don't care.

The teacher sends a student to the office with a note requesting assistance from the discipline team. A few minutes later, Mr. Boyer and two counselors walk into the classroom. The teacher briefly discusses the situation with them.

> Teacher: I'd like all students, except for Sheila, to please line up and come outside with me.

After the students have left the classroom, the administrator walks up to Sheila.

> Mr. Boyer: Sheila, we recognize you're upset and you do not want to leave the classroom. You do not have a choice in this matter. You must leave the classroom with us now.
>
> *(The discipline team escorts Sheila from the classroom.)*

A discipline support team is critical in dealing with such serious situations. Unless you know you have the support of administrators when dealing with highly difficult students, it is unlikely that you will have the confidence to set the limits they need to manage their behavior.

Exceptions to the Rules: Using Your Own Judgment

You've learned that you must be consistent in your use of consequences, that students must know that misbehavior carries with it a consequence—every time.

In most cases this guideline is absolutely correct.

In reality, however, there are going to be times when in your professional judgment it will not be in a student's best interest to provide a consequence.

Consider these situations:

- Situation #1

There is a student in your class who is usually well behaved, attentive and responsive. One day, for no apparent reason, his behavior is highly disruptive. Because this behavior is so clearly out of character, it would be much more appropriate for you to sit down and talk to this student, to try to ascertain what's wrong, than to give a consequence.

Talking with this student is a much more responsive, caring response than giving a consequence would be.

- Situation #2

You have a student in your class who has a serious problem controlling her temper. You may justifiably feel that providing a consequence at a certain moment might provoke an outburst of anger that could prove hard to handle, or disruptive to the entire class. It might be more appropriate to simply deal with the behavior at lunch, at recess or after class.

- Situation #3

One of your students is extremely upset and is crying. Providing a consequence when a student is so disturbed would be meaningless. Until the student has calmed down, there's no point in sending her to time-out, or having her write in the behavior journal.

The point of each of these examples is: Don't just blindly follow your discipline hierarchy. It is meant to guide, not control you.

In all situations you must use your professional judgment to determine which responses are in the best interests of your students. We don't live in a black and white world. Pay attention to the gray areas. Know your students and use that knowledge to guide your disciplinary responses.

Your goal is to establish a positive relationship with each and every student. If you're unsure how to respond, ask yourself, "How would I want my own child to be treated in this situation?"

Let your answer to that question be your guide.

CHAPTER TWELVE — KEY POINTS

Implementing Consequences

- Be consistent. Consequences must be provided each time a student chooses to disrupt.

- Give consequences in a firm, calm manner. The positive effects of consequences can be undermined when teachers impose consequences in a hostile manner.

- Refocus students who attempt to argue with you.

- After a student receives a consequence, take the first opportunity to recognize something positive the student is doing.

- Provide an "escape mechanism" for students who are upset and want to talk about what happened.

- "Move in" when a student is being continually disruptive.

- Stay calm if students challenge your authority.

- There are going to be times when in your professional judgement it will not be in a student's best interest to provide a consequence. Your hierarchy is a guide, not law.

CHAPTER THIRTEEN

PULLING IT ALL TOGETHER

Integrating Behavior Management and Teaching

In the previous chapters we've talked about communicating expectations, giving positive support, redirecting non-disruptive off-task behavior, and firmly and consistently using consequences when disruptive behavior arises.

Now, armed with this information, how can you put it all together?

How can you integrate all of these techniques in a manner that allows you to teach, and students to be motivated and learn?

The art of teaching is the ability of successful teachers to blend academics and behavior management efforts into a cohesive whole.

In this chapter we'll show you how to integrate these behavior management skills throughout the school day—*while* you are working with students, and *while* you are teaching academics.

Through the examples given, you will see that successful classroom management conducted by a skilled and assertive teacher is almost invisible. It is so woven into the fabric of her teaching style that an observer might not even be aware there's any strategy going on.

We will observe how in three brief classroom situations teachers can instruct their students, consistently deliver praise and positive support, redirect off-task behavior, motivate students to stay involved, and use consequences to extinguish disruptive behavior.

We will look at examples of three classroom situations at three different grade levels—K-3, 4-6, and 7-12. We highly recommend that, whatever grade level you teach, you read each of these examples. All contain points that will be useful to you. As you read, think about how you can integrate these skills into your own classroom.

In our first example, we will take a look at a primary classroom during a transition period.

Implementing Behavior Management Skills During a Transition

The scene: A second-grade classroom. It is the third week of the school year.

> The teacher rings a bell in her second-grade class. The students have learned that this signal means they are to stop, look and listen.

Teacher: Jose stopped reading.

Sean has his eyes on me.

Corrine is not talking.

Good! You all remembered what to do when I ring the bell.

It's time to get ready for recess. When I say "go," I want you to stand up, put your chairs under your desks and line up by rows at the door. Let's quickly review how you need to line up.

Tom and Juanita, can you show us all how to put your chairs under your desk, and how to walk quickly and quietly to the door?

The two students model following these directions.

Teacher: Juanita, Tom, you have a great memory for following directions. That's exactly right!

Now, when I say "go," row one will put their chairs under their desks and quickly and quietly line up. Then I will ask the other rows to go in order. Wait your turn. Wait until I tell your row to go.

All right, row one. Ready, go.

The students in row one begin to follow the direction.

Teacher: Sam, Vivian and Cynthia all remembered to push their chairs under their desks. They walked quickly and quietly to the door.

The teacher writes Sam's, Vivian's and Cynthia's names on the board under a heading marked "Classroom Superstars." As she does so, the three students beam with pride.

After writing these names, she walks over to the door, positioning herself close to where the students are lining up. She scans the room, monitoring the students as they make the transition.

Teacher: All right, row two. . .ready, go.

Anna, Rico and Lindsay are putting their chairs away and are moving quickly and quietly.

Two students from row one, Cora and Jennifer, start acting silly in line. The teacher moves over to them, stands close by and puts her hand on Cora's shoulder.

She speaks quietly to the two girls.

Teacher: Cora and Jennifer, what are you supposed to be doing?

Cora: Lining up at the door.

Teacher: That's right. Let's line up quietly then, OK?

Jennifer: OK.

Teacher: Row three. . . ready, go.

As row three begins to line up, one student, Karl, picks up a ball from the equipment bin and throws it across the room. The teacher quietly retrieves the ball and walks over to Karl. She speaks calmly to him.

Teacher: Karl, we do not throw balls in the classroom. That's a warning.

She writes Karl's name on her clipboard and then looks at the class.

Teacher: Cora and Jennifer, nice job waiting in line. Row four. . . ready, go.

After the last row has lined up, the teacher speaks to the class.

Teacher: I have a great group of listeners here. Most of you remembered to line up at the door quickly, quietly, with your hands to yourself. For such a terrific job, I think you should all applaud yourselves right now!

Let's look closer at what went on in this transition.

On the surface, the teacher gave the students a direction, and the students followed that direction. But much more occurred than that.

This teacher didn't drop her behavior management efforts for a second.

First, recognizing that it's the beginning of the year, she took the time to teach the directions she wanted the students to follow, and then took the time to have students roleplay those directions. She didn't assume her students would know or remember how to line up appropriately.

This teacher clearly understands that transitions can provide opportunity for disruption. Unless students know exactly what they are expected to do, and unless the transition is carefully monitored, a teacher can suddenly find herself with 30 students running from one activity to another.

To further prevent problems, the teacher not only taught her directions, she also used liberal amounts of positive support to reinforce students who were following those directions. Her use of positive repetition and writing names on the "Superstars" section of the board let her students know that she noticed their behavior.

Because monitoring behavior is key to managing behavior, she positioned herself in a location where she would best be able to keep tabs on most students during the transition. Therefore, when two students did go off task, she was able to easily and gently redirect them back to more appropriate behavior. Without raising her voice. Without disrupting the class.

Likewise, when a student disrupted, she wasted no time giving him a firm warning.

By using effective classroom behavior management techniques, and integrating them with sound teaching techniques, this teacher led her class smoothly through a beginning-of-the-year transition.

Now let's look in on a sixth-grade class as they move into cooperative learning teams.

Implementing Behavior Management Skills During a Small-Group/Cooperative-Learning Situation

The scene: A sixth-grade classroom. The students are about to begin a cooperative learning assignment.

Teacher: Today in your learning teams I want your groups to come up with the answers to the problems that are written on the board. Before we get started, though, let's quickly review the directions we follow when we're in learning teams.

The directions I expect you to follow are:

1. Move quickly and quietly to your team.

2. When in your team, discuss only the assignment.

3. All members participate.

4. If you need help, raise your hand.

Any questions? OK? Ready, go.

The students quickly and quietly arrange their chairs into their groups. The teacher monitors the students as they assemble.

Teacher: Very good, ladies and gentlemen. That was quick and that was quiet! And that's a point for the class towards radio time on Friday.

As the students begin to work in their teams, the teacher circulates from group to group, checking to see that everyone understands the assignment and is able to get started. As he moves from group to group, he takes a moment to offer a quick encouraging moment of recognition to each.

Teacher: That's it, Group Four. Looks like you're tackling those problems!

Group Five, nice job dividing up parts of the problem among the team.

He sits down for a moment with one group that is having some trouble understanding the assignment. As he is sitting with the group, he periodically looks up and scans the other groups. As he scans, he notices that students in Group Three aren't settling down to work.

He directs a purposeful "look" at these students, a look that lets everyone in the group know he's aware that they are off task, and that he expects them to get to work. When the students begin to work, he returns his attention to the group he's sitting with.

Teacher: OK. You're making a good start. Now let's just review for a moment how you can break this problem down.

A few minutes later, the students in Group Three stop working and begin shooting rubber bands at the group next to them. The teacher walks over to the group. He speaks to the students calmly and firmly.

Teacher: Karen, Monica, Kevin and Bobby. The directions were to work quietly with your team to come up with answers to the problems on the board. There is no shooting of rubber bands allowed in class. You all have a warning.

As he writes their names on his clipboard, the students begin loudly protesting.

Karen: Hey, we're just having fun. It's no big deal.

The teacher makes firm eye contact with Karen. His very look lets Karen know that in his classroom it is, in fact, a big deal. When he speaks, it is with firmness.

Teacher: I expect all of you to get back to work. If I have to talk to any of you again it will be after class.

Monica and Bobby begin to get to work. Kevin and Karen, however, are still acting up.

Kevin: Oh, man, why are you so hard on us?

Karen: Yeah, give us a break. You're worse than my parents.

Teacher: Kevin, Karen, you've chosen to stay after class. We'll discuss this then. I expect you to get to work immediately. If this doesn't happen, you will choose to have your parents called.

Now, I'm going to sit down with you and make sure you get to work.

The teacher sits with his students. They settle down and get to work on their assignment.

Teacher: Kevin, what are you supposed to be doing? Can you review what the assignment is for all of us?

After Group Three has settled down to work, the teacher continues to circulate among the other groups. After a few minutes, he walks back over to Group Three, leans down and speaks.

Teacher: OK. Now you're all doing a great job. I know that Group Three can work together as well as any other group in this room. Good job.

Small-group situations provide students an opportunity to work together, learn to cooperate and share responsibility. Often, though, the disruptive behavior of one or more group members can take a group off task and limit the academic value for all. As demonstrated in this example, a successful teacher must consistently monitor learning groups and provide praise, redirection and consequences if necessary.

To prevent problems from arising, the teacher in our example began by reviewing the specific directions students were expected to follow during a cooperative learning session. He made sure, even before the students moved into their groups, that these expectations were understood by all members of the class.

Once the students were dismissed to groups, he immediately implemented a classwide positive system, recognizing the students with a point toward a reward. He began circulating throughout the groups immediately, offering encouraging words and a smile as students began to get to work. A positive start for everyone.

When he noticed that one group was off task, he quickly redirected them with a "look" that let them know they'd better get to work. A few minutes later, when the off-task behavior continued, he walked over and gave a warning. They had already been given an opportunity to change their behavior. Now he was ready to follow through with a warning.

After receiving a warning, two students challenged him verbally. As you noticed, the teacher did not engage them in conversation. He did not get angry. He did not plead with them to "shape up." Instead, he followed through with his discipline hierarchy and provided a consequence, telling the students that they could discuss it later, after class.

When disruption arose, he dealt with it swiftly and firmly.

Once the consequence was given, however, the teacher sat down with these students to redirect them back to their assignment. His subsequent monitoring of their behavior resulted in praise as they eventually settled down and got to work.

The result? All students in this class were able to succeed at this lesson. Despite the disruptions that arose, this teacher's skilled use of behavior management techniques allowed him to move past the problems and enjoy a successful teaching experience.

In our final example, we will follow a ninth-grade teacher as she conducts a lecture and class discussion.

Implementing Behavior Management Skills During a Lecture/Class Discussion

The scene: A ninth-grade classroom. The students have recently returned from winter vacation and are a bit restless. We're listening in on a classroom discussion in a history class:

Teacher: We're going to continue our discussion today about the underground railroad. But before we get started, let's quickly review the directions we follow during a class discussion.

Who can give me one direction?

Students raise hands.

Teacher: Cindy? (*Teacher repeats directions as students give them.*) Eyes on teacher. Good. Sarah? That's right, raise your hand if you want to speak. Okay, Tom, what's our final direction? Notebooks and pencils out, everything else away.

Great. During our discussion I'll be looking for everyone to follow these directions. Remember, we're still working on earning points for a pizza party. When I see everyone following directions, I'll add a point to the chart.

Okay, let's get settled and ready to begin.

The students put their books away and, one by one, sit upright and pay attention.

Teacher: Bill and Ken have their desks cleared and are ready. Sarah's got her notebook out. Rebecca's ready, too. It looks like we're all set. That's a point for the class.

The teacher adds a check to her chart.

Teacher: We were talking yesterday about the underground railroad . . .

As she speaks, the teacher immediately begins circulating among the students. While she moves around the room, she makes a point of looking directly at different students. She keeps them aware of her with a smile, a nod or a look. She uses her presence and her gestures to keep the students with her.

Teacher: We've learned that the men and women who led the slaves out from the South on the underground railroad were called conductors . . .

While speaking, she notices that one student, Rodney, is looking out the window, not paying attention. Without missing a beat, she makes her way over to Rodney's desk and stands by him.

Teacher: Let's talk now about how the underground railroad functioned. Rodney, let's say you're a conductor on the underground railroad. Sue and Melissa, you're slaves who want to escape to the North. Rodney doesn't know Melissa and Sue; they've never met. How do you think the three of you could ever plan the journey? Rodney certainly can't just go over to visit Melissa and Sue, can he? Can he pick up a phone and call them? Can he send a telegram to them?

Teacher: How do you think an underground railroad
            conductor made arrangements with the slaves
            he would take north?

            Think about this question. I'm going to ask one
            of you to answer, but I'm going to expect all of
            you to comment on that answer.

*She waits a few moments for all students to consider the
question.*

Teacher: Okay. Who can tell us how Rodney, the
            conductor, would make contact with Melissa
            and Sue, slaves who want to run away to the
            North?

*The teacher waits a moment as more and more students
raise their hands.*

Teacher: Jason?

Jason answers.

Teacher: That's a good thought. Class, what do you
            think? I'd like to see thumbs up for those of
            you who agree with Jason. *(Pauses.)*

            Now thumbs down if you don't agree.

            Thumbs sideways if you just don't know.

            Chris, you had thumbs down. Why don't you
            agree with Jason's answer?

*The discussion continues in this manner as the teacher
involves all students in questions and answers.*

Teacher: Good work, everyone, on participating. That's
            another point for the class. Rodney, Melissa and
            Sue, thanks for letting us use you as examples
            on our underground railroad journey.

Now I'd like all of you to please open your notebooks and copy down the three questions that are written on the board. Write an answer to each one. No talking while you're working.

When you're finished, take out your book and begin reading in Chapter Four. The assignment is on the board. Any questions?

The teacher scans the room, moving over to Rodney. She leans down and quietly speaks to him.

Teacher: Rodney, good work getting started on the questions. You're doing great today.

Most of the students get on task. Nathan, however, isn't paying attention. Sitting next to him are two students, Rachel and Gary, who are on task. The teacher walks over to these students and quietly leans in to speak to them.

Teacher: Rachel, Gary, nice job getting right to work.

As the class begins writing, Sandy and Leo, who are seated in the back of the room, begin talking loudly to each other. The teacher walks back to them, and speaks to them in a quiet voice.

Teacher: Sandy and Leo, the rule is no shouting out in this classroom. That's a warning for both of you. The direction was to copy down the questions on the board and write your answers. Please get to work.

A few moments later, Sandy starts teasing Leo. They begin laughing and causing disruption. The teacher quickly walks back to them again.

Teacher: Sandy, Leo, this is the second time I've had to speak to you. Both of you will be staying after class to fill out a behavior journal.

Were you aware of everything that went on during this lesson? This teacher made it possible for every one of her students to start off involved and on the right track, stay involved and learn.

She was not burdened by disruption, because she has woven preventive techniques into her teaching style. She kept all of her students attentive, responsive and alert throughout her discussion. She never let students go off task, nor did she ignore a disturbance once it presented itself. At the same time her lesson never had to stop for a moment.

She orchestrated a successful lesson.

She began by reviewing specific directions. She then reinforced students following those directions by using a classwide support system, combined with positive repetition and verbal praise.

Take special note of the teaching techniques she used which allowed her to integrate behavior management so smoothly:

- She redirected an off-task student by drawing him into the discussion, giving him a "part" to play.

- She kept eye contact with students as she spoke, keeping them involved and attentive.

- When she asked questions she involved the entire class, giving plenty of time for all students to consider the question.

- She added humor to her lecture.

- She invited full-class participation through a "thumbs up," technique.

And through it all, she gave consistent praise and recognition.

When disruptive behavior did arise, this teacher dealt with it firmly. No arguments. No taking up the learning time of other students.

Was she overbearing? Did she stifle her students with negativity?

No.

This teacher demonstrates an artful balance between positive support and limit setting.

As the teachers in these three examples illustrate, classroom behavior management isn't something you learn, then put aside "in case you need it."

Behavior management skills must be with you—and utilized— throughout every teaching day, integrated into all of your interactions with students.

A smile of genuine praise, a gesture, a look, the caring tone as you speak, the effort you make to redirect behavior and the consistency with which you handle disruptive behavior—these are the skills that can make the difference between a productive, involved class and a classroom that is mired in problems.

Once you become accustomed to using behavior management skills to proactively deal with student behavior, you will find that many disruptions will never arise, and those that do can be dealt with successfully.

DIFFICULT STUDENTS

DIFFICULT STUDENTS

Consistent use of the classroom management skills presented in the previous section will enable most educators to teach 90-95% of their students to choose responsible behavior.

The remaining 5-10%—the difficult students you sometimes encounter—are the focus of this section, in which we will cover four aspects of dealing successfully with difficult students:

You know who these students are. They are the ones who may ignore your rules, may not care about the consequences of their misbehavior, and may disrupt the entire class. They are the students who argue with you, chronically disturb other students and view your classroom as a place in which to perform their own antics rather than do their work.

Besides interfering with the normal flow of classroom work, these students are disturbing to you personally. They are the ones who "push your buttons" and make you forget about being calm and assertive. They say and do things to trigger emotional responses from you that may be out of character. They may cause you to become so upset that you question your choice of profession and even seriously consider some other kind of work.

These are also the students who are hungry for attention, who most need adult guidance, positive recognition and consistent limits.

CHAPTER FOURTEEN

ONE-TO-ONE PROBLEM-SOLVING CONFERENCES

Students who are continually disruptive may need additional attention and help from you if they are to learn to manage their behavior more responsibly.

When students are continually disruptive you need to sit down and talk. You need to have a one-to-one conference.

A one-to-one conference is a meeting between you and your student to discuss a specific behavior problem. Your goal in this conference is not to punish, but to listen to the student and give caring and firm guidance.

A one-to-one problem-solving conference should be brief, lasting from a few minutes to a maximum of 10 minutes. The conference must be conducted at a time when you can give the student your undivided attention, when no other students are around to interrupt or overhear what you are discussing. Keep in mind that the purpose of this conference is to help the student choose more appropriate behavior. You are not counseling the student or taking on the role of psychologist.

When is a one-to-one conference needed?

Ask yourself, "If this were my child, would I want her teacher to sit down and work with her to help improve her behavior? Would I want her teacher to take the time and interest to show my child better options?"

If the answer is yes, then it is time to meet with the student.

Here are some basic concepts to keep in mind when you meet with a student for a one-to-one conference:

Show empathy and concern.

Your goal is for the student to gain insight into his behavior, and ultimately to choose more responsible behavior. Let the student know that you are concerned. Let the student know you care about him. Let the student know that you are not meeting to punish him but to help him.

> "I can see that you had a hard time controlling your anger in class today. I'm concerned about this because I know how difficult it makes it for you to get along with the students sitting near you. And I also know that you don't like it when I send you to time out. Let's take some time now to talk about this."

> "You and I had a really rough day. I'm concerned about that. I can see that you were really angry with me, and that you feel I'm picking on you."

Question the student to find out why there is a problem.

Don't assume you know why the student is misbehaving. Do some gentle inquiring about the problem.

> "Did something happen today to get you so upset?"

> "Are there other students who are bothering you?"

> "Do you have trouble seeing the board?"

> "Is the work too difficult for you?"

> "Is there something going on at home that's causing problems?"

Determine what you can do to help.

What can you, as a concerned teacher, do to help the student solve the problem? You may discover a simple answer that will get the student back on track.

For example:

- If a student is having trouble in class with another student, move his seat.

- If a disruptive student is seated at the back of the class, consider moving her forward.

- Contact the parents if you feel the student needs additional help and support from home.

- Boost your *positive* attention toward the student, not just your consequences. Look for the first praiseworthy behavior after the conference, then send a positive note or behavior award home.

- A student may need academic help that you, a tutor or a peer study buddy may be able to provide. Make that help available.

If you feel that any of these suggestions, or others of your own, may help the situation, discuss them with the student.

Determine how the student can improve his behavior.

Part of your meeting needs to focus on how the student can behave differently in the future.

> "I understand that you're having trouble with the other boys, but you cannot fight in this classroom. Let's talk about other ways you could deal with these situations instead. What do you think you can do, rather than fight?

> "I understand that sometimes the work is hard for you, but you have to do your work without talking. I'd like to hear some ideas from you that might help you work more quietly. Let's take a look at what you wrote in the journal."

Some students may not be willing or able to share their feelings about choosing different behavior. If this is the case, help them by pointing out the appropriate behavior. Don't react angrily or irritably to their inability to respond.

For many children, talking about behavior problems is very touchy. It's all mixed up with self-image and self-esteem. Give your support. Listen and approach the student with firm but caring resolution.

Agree on a course of action.

Combine your input with the student's input and agree upon what both of you can do to improve the situation.

> "I know that it's hard to keep from getting angry with other kids sometimes. I think your suggestion about just walking away is a good one. I'm going to help, too. Every day that you don't get into a fight, I'm going to send a note home to your parents telling them what a good day you've had.

> "I also understand that it's hard for you to work near Kevin and Stacy, so I'm going to take your suggestion and move your seat. This is a good idea, and I expect to see a change for the better."

At some point, you must clearly state your expectations to the student—that you expect him to change his behavior.

"I'm going to work with you to solve this problem. You're a good student and you're smart. I know you can behave responsibly. But remember, fighting is not allowed in class. Anytime you fight, you will be choosing to go to the principal.

"I think changing your seat will help you behave more responsibly in class. But I want to be very clear, too. If you continue talking in class, even in your new seat, you will choose to finish your work at detention."

Summarize the conference. Show your confidence!

Wrap up the conference by summarizing what was said. Most important, end with a note of confidence.

"I think we've made a good start today. I know you can do better. Starting tomorrow, it will be different."

"I'm sure you can work without talking. You've shown me that before, and I know you can show me that again."

Keep the age of the student in mind.

When conducting a one-to-one problem-solving session, you obviously must gear the discussion to make sure it is age-appropriate for the student. Follow these guidelines:

Grades K-3

Young students are very concrete. Your discussion must be very specific about how the child should behave. You may actually want to roleplay the behaviors you want the student to engage in to ensure he or she understands what you mean.

Grades 4-6

At this age students do not want to be told what to do. They want to feel they have a say in how they choose to behave. Whenever possible, involve the student in discussing how he or she should change behavior.

Grades 7-12

Most students this age do not want lectures from adults. Any problem-solving session with these students should be conducted in as matter-of-fact manner as possible. Listen to the student and invite participation.

Sample One-to-One Problem-Solving Conference—Elementary

Sandra was a capable student, but she preferred teasing and provoking her classmates to doing her work. When given a consequence, she always professed her innocence, insisting that the other students were bothering her.

For the past two days Sandra had had trouble staying on task and was getting into conflicts with students sitting near her. Her teacher had attempted to redirect her behavior, given her a warning, and sent her to the time-out area. Her behavior still wasn't improving, however, and the teacher thought more needed to be done. The last time Sandra misbehaved, the teacher had her fill out a behavior journal sheet and asked her to stay in at recess and talk.

Teacher: Sandra, I'm concerned about you. You've had a tough couple of days. I'm sure you don't like going to time out. I don't like sending you, either.

Sandra: I'm not doing anything wrong. You just always get after me.

Teacher: Do you feel I'm picking on you?

Sandra: Yeah. Juan and Roger keep bothering me and then you get mad at me when I try to tell them to leave me alone.

Teacher: Tell me about that. You wrote in the behavior journal that they were making faces at you. Is that right?

Sandra: Yes. They're always making faces at me.

Teacher: That must bother you.

Sandra: It makes me mad.

Teacher: I have an idea how I can help you. I think it would be a good idea for me to move your seat away from Roger and Juan. I would like you to change seats with Cynthia so you can sit near the front of the class. That way I can be close by you and help you with your work. What do you think about that?

Sandra: I don't care.

Teacher: Now let's look at what you need to do if someone bothers you while you are working. Can you tell me what you could do?

Sandra: Uh, well I guess I should do what I wrote about in the behavior journal. I should ignore it first. If they won't stop bothering me I should tell you.

Teacher: Yes, that might work. Now let me ask you this. What could you do if I was busy with another student?

Sandra: I guess I could just not pay attention to them.

Teacher: That sounds much better, because I expect you to do your work without arguing or disturbing the students around you. Now, what's happened the last two days?

Sandra: I had to go sit in time out.

Teacher: That's right. I don't want to keep sending you to sit by yourself, but I will if I have to. And if it continues, I'll have to call your parents. Do you understand?

Sandra: Yeah.

Teacher: Okay, after lunch we'll change your seat. And what are you going to do during work time?

Sandra: I'll do my work.

Teacher: That's a good choice. I know that you can. I'll be there to help you.

Sample One-to-One Problem-Solving Conference—Secondary

Jesse was a classic classroom clown. He had a great sense of humor, but his comments and jokes continually interrupted the teacher's lessons. He could quickly get the entire classroom in an uproar. One day he was acting particularly silly. The teacher felt it was time to have a meeting.

Teacher: Jesse, you and I have to talk. You really need to listen to what I have to say because I'm concerned about the poor choices you are making. It's not good for you. It's not good for me. And it's not good for the other kids. You're a great kid, but all the jokes and clowning around are keeping us from getting our work done.

Jesse: I'm not doing anything wrong. I'm just having fun. What's the big deal? Hey, I think you're really cool. This class is cool.

Teacher: Well, I'm glad you like the class, but your disruptions are getting in the way. I'd like to help you think of some ways to help you stop the jokes, the comments and all of the interruptions.

Jesse: Oh, man. James and the other kids, man, they really get into it.

Teacher: I understand, Jesse, but the clowning around has to stop.

If you choose to continue disrupting the class, I will contact your parents to discuss this with them. But before I do that, I'd like you to have the opportunity to make some changes yourself. Now, tell me, what will you do tomorrow instead of joking and fooling around?

Jesse: I know, don't worry. I won't mess around. I hear what you're saying. Don't call my parents.

Teacher: Good. I don't want to have to talk to you about this again, Jesse, because you know what? You really are a funny, bright kid. You make me laugh, too. That's why I want to make sure you get everything you can out of class. Your humor and attitude can work for you, not against you. You just need to learn how to use it at more appropriate times.

I'll see you tomorrow. I'm sure it will be a better day.

The one-to-one conference is designed to give both teacher and student an opportunity to calmly look at a problem situation together, and determine steps to take that will help the student choose more appropriate behavior in the future. This conference is a corrective, not punitive, action and should be looked upon as a cooperative effort on the student's behalf.

CHAPTER FOURTEEN — KEY POINTS

One-to-One
Problem-Solving Conferences

- A one-to-one problem-solving conference is a meeting between teacher and student to discuss a specific problem.

- The goal of a problem-solving conference is for the student to gain insight into his behavior and ultimately to choose more responsible behavior.

- A problem-solving conference should include the following:

  - Show empathy and concern.

  - Question the student to find out why there is a problem.

  - Determine what you can do to help.

  - Determine how the student can improve his behavior.

  - Agree on a course of action.

  - Summarize the conference.

USING POSITIVE SUPPORT TO BUILD POSITIVE RELATIONSHIPS

When dealing with difficult students, you must go beyond the guidelines of your classroom discipline plan. You must go beyond relying on the behavior management techniques that are effective with most of your students.

With difficult students, you must make a special effort to establish a positive relationship, a relationship that shows you really do care about them.

You need to show your students that you not only care about their behavior, but that you also care about them as unique individuals.

To be successful in raising students' self-esteem you may have to go beyond praising students and reinforcing them when they meet your expectations. You must also use special approaches that enable you to reach out and consistently build positive relationships with students on an individual basis.

The basis of these approaches is as simple as this: **Treat students the way you would want your own child to be treated.** With this golden rule as a guide, you will find that the more you show students you care about them, the more responsive they will be.

When students realize you do care, they won't be as likely to challenge the limits you set. They'll recognize that you're not "out to get them" and will respond to you in a more open, receptive manner.

This story illustrates what we mean:

> A few years ago we were working with a teacher who was having trouble dealing with a difficult sixth-grade boy in her class. He was very angry and withdrawn. This teacher had done an admirable job of working with him. She had praised him for his good efforts, and had set very firm limits when he was disruptive. She followed all the classic guidelines for effective behavior management, but nothing had worked for the child. She simply could not get through to him. There was a barrier between them that seemingly could not be crossed.
>
> In an effort to break through the barrier, she decided to do something she did not normally do. She invited him to eat lunch with her. During lunch, she really tried to get to know him. In the course of their discussion, the only thing he responded to, the only time his eyes lit up, was when she asked what he was interested in. His answer? His baseball card collection. When he responded, she saw a spark in his eyes she'd never seen before. Being a caring, perceptive teacher, she recognized an opportunity to chip away at the wall that stood between them. The next Monday she arranged with her brother to bring in his collection of baseball cards, which she shared with a suddenly enthusiastic boy.
>
> As she shared the cards with him, a number of other students in the class got excited—they too were interested in baseball cards. Suddenly the light bulb went off. Aha! "What if we set up a baseball-card club in class?" And you'll never guess whom she picked to be in charge—to be president of the club.

Sometimes it takes more than praise or setting limits to let kids know that you care. It takes being interested in them.

And what happened with the disruptive student in this story? The more involved he became in running the baseball-card club, the more his disruptions melted away. Soon his behavior was no longer an issue.

This student did not respond to limits. He did not respond to praise. He responded to caring and interest.

How can you show this kind of caring? What can you do?

There are no simple step-by-step answers.

Use your professional judgment and leadership abilities as you deal with each child.

Here are some suggestions that will help you develop your own collection of positive techniques.

Take a student interest inventory.

Establishing a personal relationship with students means knowing something about them personally. Be prepared.

At the start of the year take time to find out who your students are. Learn their likes and dislikes, their favorite activities, their hobbies and interests. You'll find that these insights will help you get to know your students better. And the better you know your students, the more you'll be able to reach out to them as individuals.

Here's a sample Student Interest Inventory:

Name_____

Adults who live with me:

Name_____Relationship_____

Name_____Relationship_____

Name_____Relationship_____

Brothers and Sisters:

Name_____Age_____

Name_____Age_____

Name_____Age_____

Best friends:_____

What I like to do most at home:_____

These are my favorite hobbies:_____

My favorite TV show:_____

My favorite book:_____

My favorite movie:_____

If I had one wish, I would want to:_____

When I grow up, I would like to:_____

School would be better if:_____

If I had a million dollars I would:_____

_____

What my teacher(s) did last year that I liked the most:_____

_____

What my teacher(s) did last year that I liked the least:_____

_____

Make this inventory the first homework assignment of the year. For younger kids, do it orally.

Greet students at the door.

Here's one of the best opportunities you have each day to show students you care. When they come into class, plan to be there at the door, greet them, and find something special to say to each of them. This is an especially effective way to make personal contact with those students who need your individual attention and caring words.

Here's how one high-school science teacher we worked with used this technique:

> "Every day, before the start of each period, I'm at the door. My kids probably think it's where I like to hang out, but I have a different reason for being there. As each student passes into my room, I greet them. And as I greet them I find something to say–something positive, something personal, something friendly:
>
>> 'Good job on your test yesterday, Ellen!'
>>
>> 'Glad to see you back, Mark. Hope you're feeling better.'
>>
>> 'Tom, how are you today? Great jacket!'
>
> "To put it another way, every day I start my class with every student having received some sort of positive recognition, whether it's a smile, a joke, or a statement of concern.
>
> "This isn't an accident. I make sure I'm at that door. I have it planned. I know what I'm doing and it works. I care for these kids. I know we may have some rough times once class starts, but I want each and every one of

them to know that each day is a new day, so let's start with a fresh and optimistic attitude! And for those kids who especially need some thoughtful words from me, it's a great opportunity to say something positive without singling them out in class."

Spend a few special minutes.

Sometimes the most precious and valuable gift you can give your students is your own time. Share with your students. Some of them may need special one-to-one attention that only your time and interest can offer. Spending recess or lunch with a student can make all the difference in the world to a child who needs a caring, guiding hand.

As one teacher summed it up:

> "Some kids are just needier than others. Some kids just demand more attention. Many of these kids come from homes where no one takes the time or effort to show they care. I realize that with these kids I have a responsibility to give them the special attention they need. So I give it. This is the only way I can be sure that I'm addressing their needs for a caring person in their lives, and doing everything I can to help them succeed."

Make home visits.

For some students, especially the challenging, perplexing ones, taking time to visit their homes can be extremely enlightening and helpful not only in establishing positive relationships but in gaining insight to the students' home situations. Such visits should obviously be prearranged and there may be some areas to which you won't feel comfortable going.

When talking to teachers who've taken the time and energy to make home visits, we always hear the same comments: "The time was worth it. I gained tremendous insight into the home environment, and in so doing had a better picture of the physical and emotional conditions of my students' homes."

In most cases these teachers gained great empathy for the problems and challenges the student encounters.

Make a phone call after a difficult day.

Here's a powerful positive technique to use after you've had a difficult day with a student. Students are accustomed to hearing repercussions from teachers when there's been a problem. Turn the tables and bridge the communication gap by reaching out to let the student know you care.

Here's what such a phone call might sound like:

Teacher: David, this is Mr. Jones. I want to talk to you because I feel badly about the difficult day you and I had. I don't like it when you and I have problems in class, and I could see that it wasn't easy for you, either.

Student: No, it wasn't.

Teacher: Can you give me any idea of what was going on today? Why were you so upset?

Student: I don't know.

Teacher: Is there anything I can do to help? Is there anything I'm doing that is a problem for you?

Student: Well, not really. I mean, sometimes the work's a little hard for me, that's all.

Teacher: Can you explain what you mean?

Student: Well, it's just hard.

Teacher: The next time you feel the work is too hard, let me know and I'll find a way to give you more help. How does that sound?

Student: Well, all right.

Teacher: David, I want you to know that I really want
            you to be successful in class, and I know things
            can be better. We don't have to have more days
            like we did today.

            Tomorrow we're going to start over fresh. We'll
            work to make things better. How does that
            sound?

Student: Yeah, all right. I'll see.

Teacher: OK. I'll see you tomorrow. And don't forget
            that if you're having any problems, you can
            come to me.

Make a positive phone call when a student has had a good day.

What better way to let a student know that he or she is on the right
track than by making a quick phone call to offer some well-earned
words of praise.

Here's what a positive phone call might sound like:

Teacher: Bill, this is Mrs. Williams. I've been thinking
            about class today and I just wanted to give you
            a quick call. You did such a great job working
            with your group, and I don't think I let you
            know how proud I was of you. I hope you
            realize that the contributions you made really
            helped everyone complete the assignment
            successfully.

Make get-well calls.

How do your show your concern when a friend is ill? You pick up the phone and call.

When one of your students is ill, pick up the phone and call to find out how the child is feeling. There is no quicker way to show the student, and his or her parents, that you care. When a student is ill, make a caring call. This is a good policy to follow with all of your students, but it's an especially beneficial technique to use with difficult students.

CHAPTER FIFTEEN — KEY POINTS

Using Positive Support to Build Positive Relationships

- Show students that you care about them as unique individuals.

- Greet students at the door each day. Find something special to say to each student as he or she enters the room.

- Treat students the way you would want your own child to be treated.

- Learn more about your students. Give a student interest inventory to each of your students at the beginning of the year.

- Give one-to-one attention by sharing your own time with students at recess or lunch.

- Make home visits and positive phone calls.

- Call students at home after a particularly difficult day. Let the student know you care, and that you will work with him or her to improve conditions at school.

- Make positive phone calls to students after a good day.

CHAPTER SIXTEEN

DEVELOPING AN INDIVIDUALIZED BEHAVIOR PLAN

"Every day it's the same thing. Around ten o'clock Jennifer starts bothering Max, who sits next to her. I give Jennifer a warning and she settles down for awhile. Then around eleven o'clock she'll jump out of her seat and bother someone else on the other side of the classroom. That's a check and one minute after class. And just like clockwork, after lunch she'll break another rule and have to stay two minutes after class. I don't think Jennifer cares one way or the other about receiving a consequence in this class."

When your general classroom discipline plan is not effective with a student, you'll need to establish an individualized behavior plan for him or her. Such a plan is designed to adapt the concepts of your regular classroom discipline plan to meet the unique needs of a particular student. An individualized behavior plan can help teach the student to behave responsibly and help you to develop the positive relationship with that student that so far may seem out of reach.

An individualized discipline plan will include:

- The specific behaviors expected of the student.

- Meaningful consequences to be imposed if the student does not choose to engage in the appropriate behavior.

- Meaningful positive recognition to be given when the student does behave appropriately.

Follow these guidelines when formulating an individualized behavior plan:

1. Determine the behavior(s) you expect from the student.

Select one or two behaviors to work on at a time. Choose those that you believe are most important to the child's success. (For example: Keep hands and feet to yourself; Stay in your seat unless told to get up.)

2. Decide on meaningful consequences.

Difficult students often do not respond to the basic consequences used in your discipline hierarchy. A warning, a one-minute or two-minute wait after class or time out may not be sufficient to motivate the student to choose to behave responsibly.

Often you will find the student reaches the same consequence on the hierarchy each day.

First disruption:	Warning
Second disruption:	One minute after class
Third disruption:	Two minutes after class
Fourth disruption:	Contact parents
Fifth disruption:	Send student to principal

For example, each day a student might reach the third step on the hierarchy and stay after class for two minutes. It would appear in this case that the student does not really mind staying after class and thus the consequence is not effective.

It is important to note, however, that this student *always* stops short of the consequence that involves calling the parent. In this case the teacher can conclude that it may be effective to individualize this student's discipline plan so that the first time she disrupts, instead of a warning, instead of staying after class, her parents are immediately contacted.

First disruption: Call parents

Second disruption: Send student to principal

It may be appropriate with some difficult students to provide consequences that are not on your classroom discipline hierarchy.

It may be necessary, for example, to keep a student in at recess or lunch. Or you may want the student to come after school for detention.

No matter what the consequence, it must always be one that will be meaningful to the student and, as always, provided consistently each time the student chooses to misbehave.

> Zack was a very high-strung, volatile second-grader. According to his teacher's classroom discipline hierarchy, a disruptive student was sent to the time-out area. Whenever Zack was sent there, however, he became even more disruptive, usually throwing a tantrum and upsetting the entire class.
>
> His teacher, Mr. Hawkins, recognized that Zack needed a more appropriate consequence to curb his disruptive behavior. Mr. Hawkins felt it would be better to remove Zack from the classroom and into an environment where he could calm down.
>
> With this in mind, he met with a sixth-grade teacher and arranged to have Zack go to this teacher's room to work

when he was disruptive in his own class. Mr. Hawkins then met with Zack and explained the new plan to him:

Mr. Hawkins: Zack, I know it's hard for you to control yourself, but I cannot allow you to disrupt our class, and then to yell and scream when you're sent to the quiet area. From now on when you choose to disrupt the class, you will choose to take your work and go to room 18 until you have calmed down.

Zack: I don't want to go to that class. That's a sixth-grade class.

Mr. Hawkins: Zack, I understand. But I have to find a way to help you behave more appropriately in class. It's your choice whether or not you go. If you choose to follow the rules, you will not have to go to room 18.

Zack behaved appropriately the first day after the meeting. The next day, however, he acted up and disrupted the class. An aide escorted Zack to the sixth-grade classroom. (The teacher in room 18 had instructed her students to ignore these "visiting students.")

Zack walked in, immediately started working, and, as typically occurs in an unfamiliar setting, was no problem at all while he was in this classroom. When the half hour was up, Zack returned to his own class. Upon entering the room, he told his teacher, "I don't like it in that room."

Zack chose to go to room 18 one more time that week. For him, the second time was the charm. Two visits to the sixth-grade class was sufficient to motivate him to choose responsible behavior.

The individualized plan was working because the teacher found a consequence that worked with Zack—and gave him the motivation to consider choosing more appropriate behavior.

3. Determine more meaningful positive recognition.

A natural inclination when dealing with difficult students is to "come down hard" on them. This is a shortsighted approach because the key to working effectively with difficult students is twofold:

1. Establish firmer, more meaningful consequences, *and*

2. Always balance the consequences with increased positive recognition.

Your positive recognition, as always, should begin with praise. Once you have implemented an individualized behavior plan, look for every opportunity to recognize the student's appropriate behavior.

At the elementary level, praise the student several times a day. At the middle or secondary level, recognize at least one appropriate behavior each period.

Back up your praise with other forms of positive recognition that you feel would be appropriate. Would a positive note home to the parent be appreciated? Would the student enjoy a special privilege, such as being appointed class monitor? Would the student like to earn a "no homework" pass?

Perhaps the student would benefit from—and enjoy—some personal attention from you. Would it be appropriate to have lunch with the student? Is a positive home visit called for? Or does the student just need to talk with you for a few uninterrupted minutes?

Think about it. You decide. Remember that in dealing with difficult students the balance between limits and positive recognition and support are absolutely critical.

We worked with a veteran fourth-grade teacher who in all her years of teaching had never felt the need to motivate her students with much more than a little praise and an occasional pat on the back.

The year we worked with her, however, she had a student named Raymond, an immature child who needed a great deal of attention from adults.

> Raymond was a constant problem in class, continually engaging in behavior designed to get his teacher's attention. In response to his disruptions she had been firm with him and set limits, but he continued his attention-getting behavior.

> As the disruptions continued, it became clear to her that his need for attention was greater than that of other students, and that he would get that attention one way or the other.

> Realizing this, she decided that the most positive way to help him was to let him earn her attention, not by his negative behavior, but by his positive behavior.

> She arranged for Raymond to earn time alone with her after school. For every half hour he did not disrupt he earned one minute of time with her. He could earn up to ten minutes each day. After school he would help her straighten up the room or simply sit and talk with her. Raymond immediately responded to the extra positive attention he was earning and quickly chose to eliminate his disruptions in class.

This teacher recognized that Raymond was going to get her attention one way or the other. It made sense to give him that attention for appropriate behavior rather than for inappropriate behavior.

Presenting the individualized behavior plan to a student.

Once you've formulated an individualized behavior plan you need to determine how you will present it to the student. The format of your meeting should be similar to the one discussed in Chapter 14 on one-to-one problem-solving conferences. Be firm, yet empathetic. Let the student know that you are on his side. Assure the student that you are there to help, and that you cannot allow him to engage in behavior that is not in his best interest.

> "Dennis, I can see that you're having a lot of trouble controlling your anger in class. We need to work on this because you've developed some bad habits of shouting and talking back whenever you don't get your way.

> "This kind of behavior isn't good for you, and I can't allow it to go on. I know it's not easy to change how you behave, so I am going to help you.

> "I can see that our regular classroom discipline plan isn't helping you. When I give you a warning, or have you stay after class, you don't seem to mind. Every day you receive a warning, and every day you stay after class.

> "So now I need to help you make better choices to help you stop the angry behavior.

> "From now on, the first time each day that you argue or talk back, this is what will happen: You will write on this behavior sheet what you did and what you should have done differently. This sheet will then go home to your mom for her to sign.

> "Each time you shout in class or talk back this is what you will choose to have happen.

> "Dennis, I know that it's hard for you to control your temper. And to show you how much I will appreciate the

extra effort you're going to put into controlling your temper I'm going to do the following:

"You've asked me before to send positive notes home. I know they mean a lot to you and your mom. Here's how you can earn those positive notes. Each day that you don't get angry, don't lose your temper, I'll give you a point. When you have earned three points, you'll earn a positive note to your mom."

But what if nothing works?

In our workshops we often hear teachers say that they've tried individualized behavior plans, tried contacting parents, tried sending the student to the office, but with some difficult students nothing seems to work.

When we look closely at these situations we often see a pattern similar to the one reflected in this story:

Many years ago we worked with a teacher who had a student who was angry, confrontational and talked back constantly. Throughout the semester, the teacher had usually been nonassertive in her responses to this student. She pleaded, threatened, and was inconsistent in her use of consequences.

The student in turn was consistently disruptive.

One day this student was behaving particularly badly and talked back four times to the teacher. This was the day the teacher finally reached her limit.

She took the student to the office and had her place a call to her father at work to tell him how she had behaved. After the call, the teacher sat down with the student, established an individualized behavior plan and told her, "Every day you talk back, we will call your parents."

The next day the student had **zero** outbursts.

The second day the student had **zero** outbursts.

The third day, the student talked back **one** time. The teacher informed us that she did not call the parents because "one outburst in three days was such an improvement."

The fourth day the student talked back **twice**. The teacher sat down with the girl and told her, "If you talk back again I will call your parents."

From the fifth day on the girl talked back approximately **three** times per day. (This total was just below the number of outbursts occurring daily before the individualized plan was instituted.) This time the teacher told us she did not call the parents because she felt, "It wouldn't do any good. She's just as bad as before I called. What good did calling the parents do? She's talking back again!"

This teacher used what we call a "**zero-zero-one-two-three-three-three**" approach to setting limits and providing consequences. With such an inconsistent approach the teacher is right. No consequence will work with such a student.

Let's explain what we mean.

Calling the parent *did* work! For the first two days the student chose not to talk back. The problem was that the teacher did not follow through on the third day as she had told the student she would.

The first outburst should have resulted in a phone call to the parents.

Also, just as important, on the first two days when the student did not talk back, the teacher should have provided plenty of positive recognition. She should have praised the student. A positive note should have gone home. She should have let the student know that she recognized and appreciated the effort the student was making. She should have made the student feel proud.

Instead, the student's improved behavior was ignored. She wasn't punished, but she wasn't praised either. Remember, the goal of an individualized behavior plan is to create a balance between firm, consistent limits and positive support.

In reality, nothing will work when a teacher does not consistently provide consequences to the student.

In the next chapter we will take a look at how parents and your administrator can help you work more successfully with difficult students.

CHAPTER SIXTEEN — KEY POINTS

Developing an Individualized Behavior Plan

- Develop an individualized behavior plan for students who do not respond to your general classroom discipline plan.

- An individualized behavior plan:

  1. Should include only one or two of the difficult student's most critical problem behaviors.

  2. Must establish firmer, more meaningful consequences that will motivate the difficult student to respond.

  3. Be balanced with increased positive recognition.

  4. Will work only if the teacher consistently (and without exception) provides the firmer consequences to the student.

- Positive recognition should always begin with praise.

- Difficult students will benefit from and greatly enjoy personal attention from you (lunch together, a positive home visit or phone call, an after-school conversation).

- The individualized behavior plan should be presented to the student in a firm but empathetic manner.

- Difficult students need your assurance that you care, that you are there to help and that the disruptive behavior is not in their best interest.

- An individualized behavior plan provides due process to students and parents.

CHAPTER SEVENTEEN

YOU CAN'T DO IT ALONE

Getting the Support You Need from Parents and Administrators

Parents and administrators can each offer unique support that will often have a powerful impact on students, particularly on difficult students with whom little else seems to work.

We understand, however, that it is difficult for many teachers to ask for this assistance. As we discussed in Chapter 1, the foundation of this difficulty lies in what we have called the "myth of the good teacher." According to this myth, a good teacher should be able to handle all behavior problems on his or her own and within the confines of the classroom.

Thus, if a teacher is competent, he or she should never need to go to the principal or a student's parents for assistance.

This myth places a burden of guilt on teachers—especially those who must deal with difficult students. These feelings of inadequacy tend to keep teachers from asking for the help they need with these students.

As we have pointed out, this myth is nonsense. No one teacher, no matter how skilled he is or how much experience or training she has had, is capable of working successfully with each and every student without support.

In this chapter we will focus on how you can get the support you need.

But before we look at some specific ways parents and administrators can support your efforts, let's examine what you can first do to be in the position to get that help when you need it.

First Steps to Obtaining Support

These proactive measures include:

1. Sharing your classroom discipline plan with parents and administrator.

2. When a problem arises, taking steps to deal with it on your own before asking for help.

3. Documenting a student's behavior, and the steps you have taken to handle it.

Let's look closer:

1. Share your classroom discipline plan with parents and administrator.

Parents can't support your behavioral expectations if they don't know what those expectations are. If parents are to become partners in their children's education, they must be well informed about your discipline plan. After all, contacting parents is an important part of your discipline hierarchy. If you want them to be involved when you need them, parents need to know why you have a plan, and your rationale for rules, positive recognition and consequences.

At the start of the school year, give students a copy of your discipline plan to take home to parents. In a letter, explain why a classroom discipline plan is important. Ask parents to discuss the plan with their children, sign the plan and send a signature portion back to you.

On the following page is a sample discipline plan letter to parents.

Dear Parent,

I am delighted that _____ is in my class this year. With your encouragement, your child will be a part of many exciting and rewarding experiences this academic year.

Since lifelong success depends in part on learning to make responsible choices, I have developed a classroom discipline plan which affords every student guidance in making good decisions about their behavior and thus an opportunity to learn in a positive, nurturing classroom environment. Your child deserves the most positive educational climate possible for his/her growth, and I know that together we will make a difference in this process. The plan below outlines our classroom rules, possible rewards and consequences for appropriate and inappropriate behavior. They are:

Rules:
1. Follow directions.
2. Keep hands, feet and objects to yourself.
3. No swearing or teasing.

To encourage students to follow these classroom rules, I will recognize appropriate behavior with praise, "good news" notes home and positive phone calls home. However, if a student chooses to break a rule, the following steps will be taken:

First time a student
breaks a rule: Warning

Second time: 5 minutes working away from group

Third time: 10 minutes working away from group

Fourth time: Call parents

Fifth time: Send to principal

Be assured that my goal is to work with you to ensure the success of your child this year. Please read this classroom discipline plan with your child, then sign and return the form below.

Sincerely,

- -

I have read the discipline plan and have discussed it with my child.

Parent/Guardian Signature_____ Date _____

Comments:

If you want the support of your administrator, he or she should be fully aware of exactly how you plan to deal with student behavior and under what circumstances you will send a student to his or her office. Before you implement your discipline plan, you must present it to your administrator. Explain your goals for teaching students responsible behavior and explain your rules, positive recognition and negative consequences.

You and your administrator must work together. The administrator is your ace in the hole for difficult situations.

2. When a problem arises, take steps to deal with it on your own before asking for help.

Whenever appropriate, you should attempt to handle a student's disruptive behavior on your own before you speak to the parents or administrator about the situation. Both will want to know what actions you have taken to help the student. Assure them that you have attempted to solve the problem on your own first.

Remember, your goal is to teach the student to make good behavioral choices. If you involve parents or the administrator too soon, you are not allowing the student the opportunity to change his or her own behavior.

3. Document a student's behavior, and the steps you have taken to handle it.

Early in the school year your experience and intuition will guide you in recognizing those students who may have problems as time goes on. It is vital that you begin documenting problem situations right away. Having complete anecdotal records is imperative when seeking the support of administrators and parents.

An anecdotal record should include the following information:

- Student's name and class

- Date, time and place of incident

- Description of the problem

- Actions taken by the teacher. For example:

Name: Bryan Shelby

Date: 3/16/92   Time: 10:45   Place: Yard

Problem: During recess Bryan shoved Mike Collins
               while Mike was waiting in line to play
               handball. Mike fell to the ground.

Actions taken: Bryan was counseled and then benched
               during lunch recess.

Getting Support from Parents When a Problem Arises

Now let's look at specific steps effective teachers take to get the support they need from parents when students exhibit behavior problems in the classroom.

Contact parents at the first sign of a problem.

A common complaint among parents is that teachers wait too long before contacting them about a problem. It doesn't matter whether the problem occurs the first week of school or even the first day. As soon as you become aware of a behavioral problem that parents should know about, contact them.

How do you know when you should contact a parent about a problem? Many situations are very clear: severe fighting, extreme emotional distress, a student who refuses to work or turn in homework. Don't think twice about involving parents when these situations occur.

But what about the day-to-day instances that may not be so obvious? Often you just have to use your own judgment.

If you are uncertain about contacting a parent, use the "Your Own Child" test. This test will put you in the position of the parent, and help clarify whether or not parental help is called for.

Follow these steps:

1. Assume you have a child of your own the same age as the student in question.

2. If your child was having the same problem in school as that student has, would you want to be called?

3. If the answer is yes, call the parent. If the answer is no, do not call the parent.

For example, if your child did not turn in a homework assignment one day, would you want to be called? Probably not. If your child did not turn homework in for three days in a row, however, you most likely would want to know. The "Your Own Child" test helps you treat parents the way you would want to be treated and also serves to focus your attention on problems that need parent involvement.

You will find that by using the "Your Own Child" test, you will increase your contacts with parents. And increasing contacts with parents means increasing the probability of getting parent support when you need it.

Plan what you will say before you speak to a parent.

Before you pick up a phone or meet with parents, you need to outline what you are going to say. These notes will help you think through and clarify the points you want to make. Having the notes in front of you while you're speaking will help you communicate more effectively.

Here are the points you'll want to cover:

1. Begin with a statement of concern.

Because a conference or call can be stressful and upsetting to parents, it is important that you begin the conversation by showing your concern for the student rather than just bluntly stating the problem.

> "Mr. Johnson, I care about Mark and I feel that his behavior on the yard is not in his best interest."

2. Describe the specific problem and present pertinent documentation.

Explain in specific, observable terms what the student did. If you are meeting face-to-face, show the parent your records that document the student's behavior.

> "This week Mark was involved in four fights. You can see here that he was sent to the office by yard aides twice on Wednesday and again on Thursday and Friday."

3. Describe what you have done.

Explain how you have dealt with the problem.

> "I have spoken with Mark about his behavior and he has been given detention each time he's been involved in a fight."

4. Get parental input on the problem.

Listen carefully to what the parent has to say. Here are some questions you may want to ask:

> "Has your child had similar problems in the past?" (It may be useful to examine school records to determine if the student did have problems previously and if the parent was aware of the problem.)

> "Why do you feel your child is having these problems at school?"

> "Is there something (divorce, separation, siblings, a move) going on at home that could be affecting your child's behavior?"

5. Get parental input on how to solve the problem.

Parents usually know their child better than anyone else does. They may have a good idea that could help solve a specific problem. Ask the parent:

> "What do you feel I can do to help your child?"

> "How do you feel we can work together to help your child solve this problem?"

6. Tell the parent what you will do to help solve the problem.

You've already explained what you have previously done, and what effect your actions have had. Now, let the parent know exactly what you are going to do.

> "Mr. Johnson, since this problem has continued, I am going to change the disciplinary consequences for Mark. From now on, each time he fights on the yard he will be sent immediately to the principal and you will be called.

He won't receive any warnings first, and he won't be
sent to detention."

7. Explain what you need the parent to do to solve the problem.

Just as carefully, you must explain what you would like the parent
to do to help solve the problem.

> "Mr. Johnson, we need to work together to help Mark
> improve his behavior here at school. His fights on the
> yard are completely unacceptable. It's hurting him. It's
> not in his best interest. Any time you are called about a
> fight, I'd like you to follow through at home with your
> own disciplinary measures."

8. Let the parent know you are confident that the problems can be worked out.

Well-chosen words will punctuate your message with assurance.

> "Mr. Johnson, I am confident that if we work together we
> can make this a better year for Mark. I've dealt with
> many children who have had this problem, and I can
> assure you that we will be able to turn things around if
> we are united in our efforts."

9. Tell the parent that there will be follow-up contact from you.

A parent needs to know that you are going to stay involved.
Provide this reassurance by giving a specific date for a follow-up
call or note.

> "Mr. Johnson, I am going to call you next Thursday
> evening to let you know how things are working out
> for Mark."

10. Recap the conference.

To avoid confusion and assure that your message was clear, you may need to clarify all agreements. You can do this by restating and writing down what you are going to do and what the parent is going to do. Keep this information in your files.

Teacher: We've agreed to a number of things today. Here's what I've agreed to do: I am going to change the disciplinary consequences for Mark. From now on, each time he fights on the yard he will be sent immediately to the principal and you will be called. No more warnings. No more detention.

Now, I want to be sure I was clear about the steps you're going to take. What is it that you are going to do?

Parent: Any time that I'm called about Mark's fighting, I'll take away privileges from him at home. And I'll do it every time, not just once in awhile.

Teacher: I think this is going to make a big difference, Mr. Johnson. Thank you for working this out with me. Now Mark will know that we're working together to solve this problem.

A few words about establishing a positive relationship with parents.

Most parents report that they only hear from school when there is a problem. Imagine how much easier it would be to contact a parent about a problem if you had already established a positive relationship. Instead of calling a stranger with bad news, you would be calling a parent with whom you've already exchanged good news, shared information and had other positive communication.

Establishing positive communication with all parents should be one of your priorities. It's as simple as a writing a welcoming note at the start of the year, making a phone call to relate something positive about a student or taking the time to send a note home applauding a student's effort.

Getting Support from Your Administrator

When it comes to dealing with disruptive students, an administrator can offer a teacher support that is uniquely effective.

Let's look at some ways an administrator can help you help your students.

- Reward positive behavior

- Counsel with parent and/or student

- Institute in-school suspension

- Request that parents of problem students come to school

Reward Positive Behavior

Many teachers view an administrator's role in dealing with problem students as that of the "bad guy." This is a short-sighted view. We have seen phenomenal results occur when the principal serves as a positive motivator who recognizes appropriate behavior.

A first-grade teacher once shared this story with us:

> "The principal at my school is really the foundation of my positive reinforcement program with difficult kids. In this school there is no one individual whose positive attention carries more weight or importance than the lady who sits in the big chair in the office."

This teacher rarely sent students to the office when they were a problem. She sent students to the office when they improved their behavior. She told us,

> "I'll never forget one little guy who had so much trouble controlling his anger. He really worked hard and learned to use words rather than his fists. I was so pleased that I told him he needed to make a superstar visit to the principal. At first he was afraid. Because of his experiences at his old school, he couldn't imagine a visit to the principal being fun. But he went, and he came back with a big smile on his face. A few of the principal's well-chosen words and a big hug was one of the best motivators ever for this student."

Counsel with Parent and/or Student

Have you ever had difficulty convincing a parent to come in and talk to you about a problem? We can't tell you how many times we found that a phone call from an administrator can encourage an otherwise reluctant parent to come in and meet about a problem a student is having. Likewise, having your principal sit in on a conference can demonstrate to parents how concerned the school is about their child's success and can prove a key in motivating a parent to take action in helping to solve a particular problem.

The same can be said for having the principal spend a few minutes speaking with a student about his or her behavior. The weight of the administrator's position can carry the clout necessary to let some students know that they need to choose more appropriate behavior at school.

Institute In-School Suspension

Some students' behavior is so disruptive that the administrator must remove them from the classroom. An in-school suspension room is an alternative disciplinary action to placing students on out-of-school suspension. (This option is particularly valuable in situations where students prefer unsupervised suspension at home to being in school.)

Here are some guidelines for instituting an effective in-school suspension room:

- The room must be well-ventilated and well-lighted.

- The room must be monitored at all times by an administrator, teacher, aide or other responsible adult.

- Students sent to in-school suspension must do academic work in silence. If the student disrupts the room, he or she will earn extra hours there.

- The student stays in the room for a few hours, up to a maximum of one day for older students.

- Parents should always be notified when a student receives in-school suspension.

- If there is no in-school suspension room available and the office is too distracting to students, teachers might support one another with the buddy system. Two teachers agree to provide one another, as needed, with a desk where a student will do assigned work during in-school suspension.

Note: It is very important that in-school suspension be held only in appropriate areas. Locations such as bookrooms and closets are never to be used as in-school suspension areas.

In-school suspension can prove to be one of the best support services an administrator can offer a teacher in dealing with highly disruptive students who need help in controlling their behavior.

Have the Parents of Disruptive Students Come to School

There are some students who are so defiant and so disruptive that extra efforts need to be taken to help them control their behavior. With middle and secondary students it can be very helpful to have the principal request the parent come to school and spend the day— all day—in every class with their child.

This can be a powerful action that motivates many disruptive students to choose more appropriate behavior. The parents can see exactly how the child behaves in school. More important, the student feels pressure from his peers about the parent being at school. Typically one visit by the parent is all that is necessary to motivate most students to choose to behave.

> James was an extremely defiant student. He repeatedly sent the message to his teachers that "I'll do what I want, when I want to do it." Individualized behavior plans, parent conferences, and in-school suspension all proved futile.
>
> As a last resort, the principal met with James and his mother and made it clear just how concerned he was about James' behavior. He told the mother that if James disrupted one more time he would ask her to come to school to monitor James' behavior in class—all day long. James was appalled at the idea. "No way is she coming to school!"
>
> The administrator emphasized that it was James' choice whether she came or not. If he disrupted again, she would be asked to come. Reluctantly, the mother agreed.
>
> For the next few days, James behaved appropriately. Then he tested the limits to see what would happen. As promised, the administrator called James' mother and the next day she came to school. James skulked from class to class, his mother close by. As he later said, "That was the worst thing that ever happened to me."

James made sure it never happened again. He chose to behave in a more positive manner that enabled him to be more successful in school.

CHAPTER SEVENTEEN — KEY POINTS

Getting the Support You Need from Parents and Administrators

- Parents and administrators can offer the kind of support that teachers need and difficult students respond to.

- It is a myth that teachers should be able to handle all behavior problems on their own.

- The following proactive measures must be taken by teachers in order to secure the support they need for working with difficult students.

   1. A teacher must share the classroom discipline plan with parents and the administrator at the beginning of the year.

      - A detailed letter explaining the plan must be sent to parents, with a signature portion to be returned to you.

      - Meet with your administrator to explain your discipline plan and the circumstances under which the administrator will be involved.

   2. When a problem arises, the teacher must first take steps to deal with it on his or her own.

      - Don't involve parents or the administrator prematurely. Allow the student time to change his or her behavior.

3. Factual, complete documentation of a student's behavior must be compiled, including any steps you have taken to handle the problem behaviors.

4. Anecdotal records should include:

- Student's name and class.

- Date, time and place of incident.

- Description of the problem in factual, observable terms.

- Actions taken by the teacher to handle the problem.

• Contact parents at the first sign of a problem.

• Use the "Your Own Child" test if you are uncertain whether or not the parent should be involved.

• To ensure a more productive conference, prepare an outline before speaking to a parent about a student's problem.

• Establish positive relationships with parents before problems arise through positive phone calls, notes and home visits.

• Ask for administrator involvement when counseling with parents and/or student about problem behaviors.

• Institute an in-school suspension program for extremely disruptive students.

• Ask parents of problem students to spend an entire school day with their child. Peer pressure makes this an extremely uncomfortable situation for defiant, disruptive students.

GOING BEYOND

It has been our goal in this book to provide you with a solid foundation upon which you can establish a classroom where you can teach and your students can learn—a classroom that addresses the individual needs of each student and the individuality of you, the teacher.

To this end, the concepts presented here are part of an ongoing process, not the final word.

We find that teachers who are most effective in dealing with student behavior, in raising student self-esteem and in increasing students' potential for academic success often go beyond the concepts presented in this book. They take the Assertive Discipline skills and techniques they've learned with them into their classrooms, then adapt them to their own personal teaching style and to the unique needs of their students. In addition, they often integrate our concepts with other theories and approaches to managing student behavior.

For example:

> There are teachers who do not determine the rules for their classroom by themselves. Instead, they involve students in the decision-making process and periodically ask the entire class to evaluate the rules to see how effective they are.

> We also hear from teachers who involve students in teaching one another classroom rules or specific directions. In some cases, teachers assign one or two students to be behavior monitors. When new students are enrolled in the classroom they are taught the rules by the behavior monitors rather than by the teacher.

Other teachers we have worked with hold class meetings when they feel they are providing too many consequences. At these meetings, they ask the students to give feedback on how problem situations might be handled more appropriately with actions other than negative consequences.

It is the flexibility that is built into Assertive Discipline that allows teachers to effectively meet the needs of all types of students.

We also know of teachers who incorporate other classroom management theories and approaches into their Assertive Discipline efforts. This is perfectly acceptable. It is the professional responsibility of any educator to analyze, synthesize, critique and adapt the various behavior management theories available. It is only through this process that your own teaching style will evolve, and your ability and confidence to handle the many classroom challenges will increase.

Here's what we mean:

Many behavior problems can be eliminated by changing instructional strategies. For example, teachers who have difficulty managing student behavior when lecturing in front of the class often report that they experience fewer discipline problems when students work and study together in cooperative learning groups.

It's often difficult to keep today's "MTV" generation of students attentive, interested and motivated in class. By learning to create more relevant and stimulating curriculum, teachers can cut down on student boredom and the resulting disruptive behavior.

Many of today's students can benefit from individual assistance. There are many social skills training and counseling programs available that are designed to give a teacher the skills necessary to establish individualized behavior plans for even the most difficult students.

Behavior problems in class are often the result of conflict between students. Teachers often report that conflict resolution programs, designed to give students skills to resolve conflicts among themselves, have had a positive impact on reducing behavior problems in the classroom.

Your students deserve the best you can give them. For some students that means seeking answers from a variety of resources.

When all is said and done, it is our hope that your continuing efforts to provide the optimum classroom environment for your students do not end when you close this book. Your constant efforts are needed to ensure that your classroom is an active learning environment. When the time comes to alter or change an approach, you need the skills to do so and the confidence to proceed.

Above all, never forget the power and impact you can have with children. We'd like to present you with a quote from Haim Ginott's *Teacher and Child* that appears in our original text—a quote that still has a profound impact upon us and is well worth repeating.

> "I have come to a frightening conclusion. I am the decisive element in the classroom. It is my personal approach that creates the climate. It is my daily mood that makes the weather. As a teacher I possess tremendous power to make a child's life miserable or joyous. I can be a tool of torture or an instrument of inspiration. I can humiliate or humor, hurt or heal. In all situations it is my response that decides whether a crisis will be escalated or de-escalated, and a child humanized or dehumanized."

In closing, to underscore both the impact and responsibility each teacher has, we leave you with a thought we read years ago, one that continues to motivate our efforts each day:

> *Children are our hope for the future. But we are the hope for theirs.*

Additional Readings
in Behavior Management

Albert, L. *Cooperative Discipline*. Circle Pines, Minnesota: American Guidance Service, 1991.

Brookover, et al. *Creative Effective Schools*. Holmes Beach, Florida: Learning Publications, 1982.

Charles, C. M. *Building Classroom Discipline*. New York: Longman, 1989.

Dinkmeyer, D. *Systematic Training For Effective Teaching*. Circle Pines, Minnesota: American Guidance Service, 1979.

Doyle, W. *Classroom Management*. West Lafayette, Indiana: Kappa Delta Phi, 1980.

Dreikurs, R. Grunwald. *Maintaining Sanity in the Classroom*. New York: Harper and Row, 1971.

Englander, M. *Strategies For Classroom Discipline*. New York: Praeger, 1986.

Evertson, et al. *Classroom Management for Elementary Teachers*. Englewood Cliffs, New Jersey: Prentice Hall, 1984.

Jenson, W., Sloane, H., and Young, K. R. *Applied Behavior Analysis In Education: A Structured Teaching Approach*. Englewood Cliffs, New Jersey: Prentice Hall, 1988.

Jones, F. *Positive Classroom Discipline*. New York: McGraw Hill, 1987.

Jones, V., and Jones, L. *Comprehensive Classroom Management: Motivating and Managing Students*. Needham Heights, Massachusetts: Allyn and Bacon, 1990.

Kreidler, W. *Creative Conflict Resolution*. Glenview, Illinois: Scott, Foresman and Company, 1984.

McGinnis, E., and Goldstein, A. P. *Skillstreaming the Elementary School Child*. Champaign, Illinois: Research Press Company, 1984.

Morgan, D., and Jenson, W. *Teaching Behaviorally Disordered Students*. Columbus, Ohio: Merrill Publishing Company, 1988.

Morrow, G., MA. *The Compassionate School: A Practical Guide to Educating Abused and Traumatized Children*. Englewood Cliffs, New Jersey: Prentice Hall, 1987.

Paine, et al. *Structuring Your Classroom For Academic Success*. Champaign, Illinois: Research Press Company, 1983.

Seeman, H., Ph.D. *Preventing Classroom Discipline Problems: A Guide for Educators*. Lancaster, Pennsylvania: Techomic Publishing Company, 1988.

Lee and Marlene Canter are well known for their work in the fields of education and parenting. Together they developed three nationally recognized professional development programs: Assertive Discipline®, Parents On Your Side® and Homework Without Tears®. They have written over 40 books and produced more than 10 video programs geared to helping educators and parents raise happy, responsible children.

Prior to founding Lee Canter & Associates in 1976, Lee Canter pursued a career in social work, working with child guidance agencies throughout California. Marlene Canter began her career as a resource specialist focusing on teaching students with special needs.

Today Lee and Marlene manage Lee Canter & Associates, a company dedicated to researching and developing innovative and effective programs that help educators and parents work together to improve the quality of education for children everywhere.

Over the past 15 years, Lee and Marlene Canter and their staff have trained over 1,000,000 educators and parents. Articles about Lee Canter have appeared in major educational publications as well as in *Newsweek*, *U.S. News & World Report*, the *New York Times* and the *Los Angeles Times*. Lee is frequently a featured speaker at national educational conferences and has made numerous television appearances, including the "Today Show" and "Oprah Winfrey."

Lee and Marlene, both native Californians, reside in Los Angeles with their two children, Josh and Nicole.

MATERIALS FOR TEACHERS
from Lee Canter & Associates

Succeeding With Difficult Students™

CA2525 Succeeding With Difficult Students Text, Gr. K–12

CA2527 Succeeding With Difficult Students Wkbk, Gr. K–12

Assertive Discipline®

CA1000 Assertive Discipline Text (revised edition)

CA1001 Assertive Discipline Elementary Workbook, Gr. K–5

CA1003 Assertive Discipline Middle School Workbook, Gr. 6–8

CA1005 Assertive Discipline Secondary Workbook, Gr. 9–12

CA1009 Assertive Discipline for Parents

CA1010 Parent Resource Guide

CA1018 Seasonal Motivators

CA1026 Teacher's Mailbox

CA1029 Back to School with Assertive Discipline

CA1033 Desktop Motivators, Gr. 1–4

CA1034 Awards for Reinforcing Positive Behavior, Gr. 1–3

CA1035 Awards for Reinforcing Positive Behavior, Gr. 4–6

CA1042 Bulletin Boards for Reinf. Positive Behav., Gr. K–3

CA1043 Bulletin Boards for Reinf. Positive Behav., Gr. 4–6

CA1048 Positive Reinforcement Activities, Gr. K–6

CA1052 Positive Reinforcement Activities, Gr. 7–12

CA1053 Schoolwide Positive Activities

CA1061 Monthly Citizen Slips

CA1063 Teacher's Plan Book Plus #2

CA1064 Teacher's Plan Book Plus #1

CA1073 In Our Classroom Poster, Gr. K–3

CA1074 Classroom Rules Poster

CA3017 Record Book Plus

Parents On Your Side®

CA2004 Parents On Your Side, Gr. K–12

CA2010 Parents On Your Side Workbook, Gr. K–8

CA2033 Teacher's Plan Book Plus #4

Homework Without Tears®

CA1205 Homework Without Tears—Parent Guide

CA1211 Homework Without Tears for Teachers, Gr. 1–3

CA1212 Homework Without Tears for Teachers, Gr. 4–6

CA1213 Homework Without Tears for Teachers, Gr. 7–12

CA1223 Homework Organizer for Students, Gr. 4 –8

CA1225 Homework Motivators, Gr. 1–6

CA1231 Creative Homework, Gr. 1–3

CA1232 Creative Homework, Gr. 4–6

CA1233 Creative Homework, Gr. 7–12

CA1241 Practice Homework, Gr. 1–3

CA1242 Practice Homework, Gr. 4–6

CA1247 How to Write a Research Paper, Gr. 5–8

CA1248 How to Study and Take Tests, Gr. 5–8

CA1249 How to Use the Library, Gr. 5–8

CA1250 How to Write Better Book Reports, Gr. 5–8

CA1260 Teacher's Plan Book Plus #3

For the location of your nearest school supply store or to request a free catalog, contact Lee Canter & Associates.